The Art of Spiritual Rock Gardening

The Art of

# Spiritual
# Rock Gardening

Donna E. Schaper

illustrations by
Simon Dorrell

HiddenSpring

Library of Congress Cataloging-in-Publication Data
Schaper, Donna.
The art of spiritual rock gardening / by Donna E. Schaper; illustrations by Simon Dorrell.
p. cm.
ISBN 1-58768-005-X
1. Rock gardens. 2. Gardening—Religious aspects. 3. Schaper, Donna. I. Title.
SB459 .S29 2001
635.9'672—dc21                                    2001024096

Published by
HiddenSpring
an imprint of Paulist Press
997 Macarthur Boulevard
Mahwah, New Jersey 07430
www.hiddenspringbooks.com
Printed and bound in the
United States of America

# Contents

# Stone

# Plants

# Why Stones in the Garden?

This book blends the spiritual and practical parts of rock gardening. Those who think they "can't" garden will receive inspiration and instruction in how to begin. Those who think they aren't the spiritual types will find that the so-called spiritual is not nearly as unachievable as their fears imagine it to be. The book resembles a Russian nesting doll in which one part holds a smaller part, which then holds an even smaller part, or spiritual within practical within spiritual within practical, as though they were actually a piece of each other, which they are.

This book is good for either the novice or the experienced gardener, for people just beginning a spiritual journey, or for those well on the way. It is a modest appreciation of stones and gardens and what they mean to the human spirit.

I call its way *nonelaborate*—precisely because labor is what is eliminated in its method. Laboring in the garden is abusive to the garden; laboring on the Spirit is an insult to the Spirit. Each is freer and simpler than our fears allow us to see. What are these fears? They are well-tutored illusions: We aren't good enough for good things. We aren't smart enough for beautiful things. We don't work hard enough for the lovely to be a part of our lives. Stones and spirit simplify these fears: They caress them. They give us permission to be good and beautiful, lovely and even loving of ourselves. Rock gardening is a way to love stone and spirit simply. It is not elaborate.

In this nonelaborate method, we spiral to a spiritual simplicity. We garden simply. We pray in the garden simply. We don't follow a lot of rules or recipes; we don't care as much about doing things the "right" way as we care about doing things in a simple, fun, or beautiful way. We get out of our way and into *our* way. We layer the garden and our spiritual development in the Russian nesting method. We let things connect, and in those connections we find a way to garden and to pray.

In this book, we take the work out of spirituality and gardening. We insert the play. We play at prayer in the garden. We play at work in the garden. We see how the practical effort of digging is connected to the spiritual effort of digging. Or staking. Or hauling. Or weeding. Or pruning. Or rolling stones around the landscape. Physical acts are spiritual acts, but they are still physical acts. We play our way to piety—that old-fashioned word for spirituality.

Each of the pieces are short, guided lessons in gardening and spirituality, or piety. Each can be read alone, as daily devotionals throughout the stone season (which can be any season), or they all can be read in one session in order to get a jump start into the world of rock gardening. Gardening and spirituality like to offer us these kinds of options all the time. These choices constitute an important spiritual message. Not every piece might be for you; several will have your name written all over them. Some pieces will be sneakily practical; others sneakily spiritual.

Don't make the garden that doesn't appeal to you. Find the one that does and adore that garden.

# SPIRIT

Stone-cutters fighting time with marble,

you fore-defeated

Challengers of oblivion

Eat cynical earnings, knowing rock splits,

records fall down,

The square-limbed Roman letters

Scale in the thaws, wear in the rain.

The poet as well

Builds his monument mockingly:

For man will be blotted out, the blithe earth die,

the brave sun

Die blind, his heart blackening:

Yet stones have stood for a thousand years,

and pained thoughts found

The honey peace in old poems.

—Robinson Jeffers
"To The Stone-Cutters"

# Driving Their Stone Home

Once I started seeing stones, I couldn't get my eyes off of them. I knew they were there at the base of the Catskill Mountains in New York State, where I was born. They were for climbing or for picnics or as settings for our various plays. (They were the supporting cast, not the major actors.) Stones are everywhere, and once we bring them to consciousness, they stay.

My preoccupation with stones may have begun with my parents' tombstone. It was not my idea to drive my parents' tombstone north. It was my mother's idea—and one that suits her well. She is a master at coupon-clipping and can go to the grocery store and buy $25 worth of groceries for $5. Sometimes, the stuff she buys is a little odd—we are still using up the creamy Alfredo sauce from her last expedition.

She is not the kind of woman who would leave a $500 tombstone—paid for on time just to get a discount—abandoned in South Carolina after she had buried her husband in his home state of New York. In addition, we were the kind of family that knew the highway north and the highway south well. We even had a favorite pancake place (Silver Dollar on Rt. 83 outside of Harrisburg, Pennsylvania) and knew the best motel (South Hill, just over the Virginia border). We had made the trip for death before—for her mother, for his stepfather—and sometimes for Christmas, too. "Stony the road we trod" is a phrase we might have borrowed from the slaves, which we were not, even though we did bow to many thrift-causing masters—notably the garment industry, which "employed" my father.

We began our move south when I was eleven, when my father decided not to be a part of the growing labor movement in the garment industry. He chose "management," a decision that probably did put me through college and also caused him to be fired a few days before his sixtieth birthday so that the real management didn't have to pay out his pension. If he had stayed union, stayed north, and stayed focused in his anger on the right subjects, perhaps we could have been poor but proud. Instead, we became middle class and were humiliated. I have the B.A. and the stories to prove it.

Every year after our initial move south, we were moved from one small southern town in South Carolina to another so that my father could train black women in sewing-machine operations. I went to a different school every time we moved.

By then, though, the schools, as bad as they were, couldn't help me with my prejudices: I had become a rank ideologue on the whole matter of the South. I hated it. It had uprooted me. It was the kind of place where you had to be buried with strangers, next to their stones, as opposed to the kind of place Kingston, New York, had been. There you could put your stone in with people who knew you so well that they would comment on its size and shape. Once our family was uprooted, we were in with people who didn't seem to care as much or as badly as those in Kingston.

Ideology always brings punishments—and here, I thought, was mine. I got to drive the stone north. My brother had the privilege of driving Daddy's ashes north. I was jealous.

The punishment proved putative, all threat, little reality. My therapist cautioned against the "spooky," and my friends just kept staring at me. My children simply shook their teenage heads; only my oldest was supportive. I was not only driving my parents' tombstones, with his name and her name carved right on it, with his dates completed and hers not, but I was also driving their car north. My mother had given it to her grandson, my eldest son, who got his permit a few days before I flew south to pick up the stone. People say he was watching out the window for the car to show up. People also say that there was a distinct disappointment in his eyes when he saw the 133,000-mileage-old Chevrolet Cavalier arrive in the driveway. He never inquired about the disposition of the stone: He was looking at new life, not fresh death. New life was brown, rusty, and had four doors.

The car had sat in the garage in North Carolina for over a year as my parents had inched their way north in retirement. My mother had left my father three months before his death

—this time for good. She had left him before but always had gone back. He was the kind of guy who couldn't insure a car— so rich was his driver's rage and his penchant for attacking the state police. She was the kind of woman who stuck with her man for fifty-three years—for richer and for poorer. Finally, she had had enough and left for parts north. Three months later, her husband was dead. He died alone; his body not found for four days. My brother discovered him eventually. By the time my father died, he had driven everyone off. He was alone. The death was so sad that it made the separation/divorce look easy. Something was needed to mark the end of this north-south story.

We buried my father with his father in Kingston. No stone. No marker. Just incoherent grief. No one spoke of the obvious question—which is whether my mother would choose to be buried with her parents, up on the stony hill, or with my father and his father.

It took her a year to decide. When she did, I flew south to pick up the stone that has both of their names on it. We will move his ashes to a place where they can be buried together. Fifty-three years of marriage is not wiped out by three angry months of separation, thus says the stone.

I am going to plant a weeping cherry tree on their graves when the stone is finally set and the rest of this north-south story is over. Isaac's "new" car has just a little red South Carolina dirt in it, left over from the gravestone's tenancy. Otherwise, it is ready to drive.

Gardening with stones is one legacy of this tombstone: I am more desperate than most people for beauty. That desperation is my urgency. I am a stone gardener because of all that stones have taught me.

# Rocks

We all have relationships with rocks. Rocks were the first tools and the first weapons: They have been used throughout history by people to act with intention on our environments. Whether as my parents' tombstone and me or as Helen and Scott Nearing hauling stone for decades to build their own "good life" house or as the Irish building altars or cairns in the fields or even as the slang of being caught between a rock and a hard place or on a slippery slope, rocks *mean* a lot to people. We don't need the exotic or the rural or the ancient to be awed by stones: A city street can demonstrate the beauty of rock in a pocket garden or in a stone that is just lying on the ground. Rocks mean different things to different people. They often mean deep things.

If you need a more devotional spot in your garden or on your block, rock is the way to go. You can make your own seat from rock and your own symbolism. You may want to review vows on its site, or you may want to let its symbolism be decided by whoever uses it. If a spiritual garden is your destination—a site that is beyond the upturned bathtub showcasing a religious figure still popular in a pious America and beautiful in its own special way—stone is the direction you'll want to take.

Even if you live in an apartment and don't have a garden, you, too, can have a rock garden. You may already have one. Many people place rocks artistically on their mantels or inside their potted plants. Many cluttered kitchen counters seem to have a rock or two on them, just for something round and good for the cook to feel and fiddle with, something unbreakable to lord over all the junk mail. Rocks appeal to people: We like to touch them and observe them and keep them close by.

My main garden is in the northeast; yours may be on the ocean or in the desert or in a swamp or on a mountainside. Rocks vary region by region in their size, shape, density, and abundance, but they are used in every region as a way to elicit a little art from nature.

In the yard of a modest home just down the block from mine, a homeowner has built a circular rock wall that encloses a working stone fountain. Why did someone do this in a tiny yard? Why did another make art out of pebbles on the beach? Why? Because that is what people do with rock. We shape it. We shape it in ways that let it suggest something to us. Gardeners are people who interfere with nature, someone wise said. Artists do the same. Why not interfere with rocks?

A local sculptor created one of his rock piles in a mountain stream to look like a congregation worshipping a waterfall. He could have done almost anything. That waterfall was there to be worshipped! He couldn't move the waterfall; he couldn't change its course. He could, however, decorate it; he could deepen it. He took literally dozens of rocks and played with their colors and shapes such that the whiter ones became the heads of the "parishioners" and the darker ones their bodies. The physics of stacking them could not have been easy, but there they were, looking as if one stone belonged to another the way your head belongs to your body. There was a congregation of forty or so rock figures arranged in small groupings so that they looked a bit like families. The rocks are perfect "clay" from which to form pictures: They are both sturdy and flexible.

We like rock and its combination of flexibility and sturdiness. We like what we can do with it and what we can't do with it. Its possibilities are acquainted with its impossibilities in a good rock garden.

People who live by the water know rock quite intimately. I am thinking of Goat Rock at the mouth of the Russian River in California, two hours north of San Francisco. Someone has put thousands of clusters of hen-and-chickens in the crevices of that enormous rock, and these small plants have thrived there—as small and intricate as Goat Rock is large and plain. On Montauk Point on Long Island, the tides reveal not just shells but deep blue-and-gray stones, well polished by their sea voyage.

The uses of rocks in the garden and in "unblemished" nature—a nature not "messed with" or interfered with—are many. Some rock gardens happened because no one touched the rocks, and plants grew up around them. These gardens are to be enjoyed; that is their use. If a gardener is someone who interferes with nature, that very activity implies that a gardener can also choose not to interfere. There are "made" gardens, and there are natural gardens. We make rock gardens, and we find rock gardens. Both can be wonderful sights and sites for beauty and meditation.

The rock garden is a multifaceted matter. There are lots of parts to it—siting it, preparing the soil, getting rid of the rocks you don't want and finding the ones you do, weeding it, changing it, and leaving it alone to go fallow. More often than not, getting rid of some stones on behalf of others is the art of stone gardening.

The meaning of rock gardens is often in the coalescence and combination of many facets: Their truth is the process of building them slowly and meditatively over time and watching them change. Their nub is the interaction of our freedom to move rocks within the limits that the gardens have imposed already on their sites. Even Goat Rock will change. Process over product, journey over destination, a work in progress— these are the long-term joys of building a rock garden. It never finishes nor does it have to. It also will last long after you are gone unless it topples in a bad storm the way my artist

friend's waterfall worshippers did one day. Nature is not just
an object in rock gardening; nature is also the subject. Nature
acts and also is acted upon. Nature can be moved, and nature
cannot be moved; movement depends on mood and physics
together—not on either but on both.

If you have a rock in a garden or a rock garden or an
arrangement of rocks or plants on a table or a mantle or a
favorite rock in your local park, you can call yourself a rock
gardener. You have interfered with nature and rearranged it.
You may also call yourself a spiritual rock gardener because
you have a place to go whenever you need to pray or curse or
think or just sit and remember. You have a place for the desperation you feel for beauty. The rocks help.

Rocks are a mixed blessing; they have a sadness as well as a
joy to them. Ask any tombstone: Does it stand for death or
eternal life? New England farmers had to move heavy stones
in order to eat. They would be more than a little amused at
the current trend of "gentle man and woman" farmers hauling rock back onto their land. New Hampshire granite meant
people couldn't grow anything on a lot of the land that they
paid good money for. Rocks are cold and hard and mean if
you stub your toe against them. They are also strong enough
to shelter a large spiritual experience. Why rocks? Because
they are capable of all we experience and more.

# Rocks of Ages

"Rock of Ages," we are told, is "cleft for me." The old hymn goes on, "Let me hide myself in Thee." A rock garden is a place to hide and a place to be cleft, and the very rocks are large enough to contain much of our human experience, both the joy and the sadness. When we create little "domestic" rock gardens, we are imitating a grand and large human history. We connect rock with ages.

Interestingly, "Rock of Ages" was composed out of economic, rather than spiritual experience. Augustus Montague

Toplady wrote this poem in 1776 to liken the burden of the English national debt to the burden of sin. (In 1830, Thomas Hastings wrote "Toplady," which later became the music for the poem.) The rock in the song was offered as solace to both real sin and real debt. Most people don't have to go far from home to know genuine sin and genuine debt. Rocks are large enough for the experience of each—and more. Rocks cleave. They hide. They secure. They connect the economic to the spiritual, the tough to the gentle, the difficult to the easy: They are large enough to contain the full range of human and spiritual experience.

What we do with rocks in our little gardens connects us to people around the world. We bond with those who built Egypt's pyramids, England's Stonehenge and Avebury, Europe's great cathedrals, America's pre-Columbian temples, Africa's ancient cities, and dolmen in Wales and Ireland. Stones are an essential part of Zen gardens and at the core of the Japanese art of Suiseki and viewing stones. Early Irish mounds, going back to the time of St. Patrick, are made by the rocks people piled to measure time, adding stones year after year. Jews place small rocks on tombstones to express both grief and remembrance. Gravestone rubbing, or getting the art off the stone, remains a popular weekend pastime in New England.

When Muslims reach Mecca, they circumambulate seven times counterclockwise around the Ka 'aba, where the Black Stone (the symbol of the original covenant between God and humanity) is embedded. The Black Stone is said to have descended from heaven as a sign of the covenant. Pilgrims who have trouble walking are carried on a palanquin. When they come to the corner of the Black Stone, they hold up their hands in order to receive the *barakah*, or blessing, from the

stone. The casting of stones at the devil also is a requisite part of the *hajj,* or pilgrimage, to Mecca.

Rocks bind us to a world of cultures. John Lane Deer, a Sioux medicine man, reminds us that *Inyan,* or rocks, are holy. Sui Jianguo, a Chinese artist, speaks of the "versatility of rock as material and metaphor." About ten years ago, he created a grouping of boulders encased in a mesh of corrugated steel rods. This monumental reconstruction of nature took two years to complete. Some of us go grand; others go simple. Many use rock.

The Jews certainly knew about rocks. The Ten Commandments came on stone. Water comes from the rock in the desert. The traditional Jewish hymn "Maoz Tsur Y'shuati," or "Rock of Ages," is sung during Hanukkah. "Rock of Ages, let our song praise your saving power; you, amid the raging foe, were our sheltering tower . . . ."

Instituted by Judas Maccabeus and the congregation of Israel in 165 B.C.E., Hanukkah commemorates the rededication of the temple in Jerusalem after the Jewish victory over Antiochus Epiphanes. The temple was destroyed; the temple was rebuilt. This experience is the one we have in our rock gardens as well as in our wars. We thrive. We are destroyed. We thrive again. We hide. We come out of hiding. When we come out of hiding, we are strengthened. The stones come together in a sacred site; the stones fall apart as a sacred site. Even temples collapse. Rock gardens are places we go to hide so that we can resurface. Rocks and rock gardens have long stood for the rising and waning of life, the comings and goings, the ups and downs.

The rocks of Jerusalem tell all of these stories and more: Golgotha and the rock that the angels rolled away for Jesus join the Muslim Rock of the Dome and the destroyed and rebuilt temples. These wailing walls of history tell thousands of other stony reminders of ascent and descent—of weeping that lasts for a night so joy can return in the morning.

Mt. Moriah is the site of a single bare rock around which many of these stories cohere. It was originally considered highly sacred for two reasons: An ancient Semitic tradition stated that the bare rock atop the mount was held in the mouth of the serpent Tahum and that this place was the intersection of the underworld and the upper world. It was also considered to be the site where Abraham had built an altar on which he prepared to sacrifice his son Isaac.

Two temples of the Jews on this site were followed by the Jupiter temple of the Romans. Later, the Muslims came to Jerusalem and had their time of religious residence. The site was the very same rock where previously had stood the Jupiter temple. The reason (more fundamental to the Muslims than the mere political expediency of seizing another religion's sacred site) was based on a passage in the Qur'an, which was interpreted by the faithful as linking the prophet Muhammad with Jerusalem and the Temple Mount. That passage, the seventeenth Sura, entitled "The Night Journey," relates that in a dream or a vision Muhammad was carried by night " . . . from the Sacred Mosque to the farthest Mosque, whose precincts We did bless, in order that We might show him Our Signs. . . ." Muslim belief identifies the two mosques mentioned in this verse as being in Mecca and Jerusalem. According to tradition, Muhammad's mystic night journey was in the company of the Archangel Gabriel, and he rode on a winged steed called El Burak, meaning lightning, which had the face of a woman and the tail of a peacock. Stopping briefly at Mt. Sinai, another great stone place, and Bethlehem, they finally alighted at Temple Mount in Jerusalem and there encountered Abraham, Moses, Jesus, and other prophets, whom Muhammad led in prayers. Gabriel then guided Muhammad to the pinnacle of the rock, which the Arabs call *as-Sakhra,* where a ladder of golden light materialized. On this glittering shaft, Muhammad ascended through the seven heavens into the presence of Allah, from whom he received instructions for himself and his followers. After this divine encounter, Muhammad was flown back to Mecca by Gabriel and the winged horse, arriving there before dawn.

At this site hallowed by people of so many faiths, Omar's successor, the tenth Caliph, Abd alMalik ibn Marwan, built the great Dome of the Rock between C.E. 687 and C.E. 691. Often incorrectly referred to as the Mosque of Omar, the Dome is not a mosque for public worship but rather a *mashhad,* a shrine for pilgrims. (Adjacent to the Dome is the al-Aqsa Mosque wherein Muslims make their prayers.) Designed by Byzantine architects engaged by the Caliph, the Dome of the Rock was the greatest monumental building in early Islamic history and remains today one of the most sublime examples of artistic genius that humanity has ever produced. Writing of the beautiful structure with its heavenly dome, its columns of rare marble, and its brilliant mosaics, the British authority on Muslim architecture, K.A.C. Creswell, exclaimed:

> Under a scheme whereby the size of every part is related to every other part in some definite proportion . . . the building instead of being a collection of odd notes becomes a harmonious chord in stones, a sort of living crystal; and after all it really is not strange that harmonies of this sort should appeal to us through our sight, just as chords in music appeal to our hearing. Some of the ratios involved . . . are fundamental in time and space, they go right down to the very basis of our nature, and of the physical universe in which we live and move.

For two millennia the control of the city's primary sacred places has shifted frequently between the three monotheistic religions of Judaism, Christianity, and Islam.

The energy, or presence, of the sacred is not monopolized by any of these faiths but rather gives rise to each of them.

This sacred presence accumulates intensity over time. We may speak about these sites and the many other pilgrimage destinations in Jerusalem as containers of the accumulated spirit of holiness. That spiritual energy has been enriched over many centuries, like fine wine in a wooden cask, and it radiates today throughout the city of Old Jerusalem.

In the Dome of the Rock, beneath the ancient sacred stone, is a cavelike crypt known to the Muslims as Bir el-Arweh, the Well of Souls. Here, according to the faithful, the voices of the dead may sometimes be heard along with the sounds of the rivers of paradise.

If you listen deeply in your own garden, sometimes you can hear them, too.

# Rock and Roll

If you were born at a certain time in human history, you love rock and roll. The music comes on, and you start to boogie. You can't help but remember the fun of flabbergasting your parents or of finding deep rhythms in your hips and arms and legs that you didn't really know you had. You like rock and roll.

Interestingly, rock and roll is the beginning of the postmodern war between stability and fluidity. Rolling the rocks, pushing the stability, bursting the envelope, and thinking outside the box—all of these actions find their hymns in rock and roll.

Jesus rolled the rock, or so some folk singers like to argue. He busted the stone and stability that was in his way, and he burst from the tomb. Some people call this humiliation of the rock "resurrection."

What people like about having stones in their gardens is the way the stones are eternal and sturdy and everlasting and full of reminders of the old-fashioned God—the one who did not boogie. What people also like about having stones in their gardens is the rock and roll—the humor of the God who does, and can, move powerfully in hips and history.

Once you have made a rock garden or put a rock in your yard or rocked your garden, you also can roll it to another place. You can change your rock's habitation.

Rocks are good for the garden because they are good for the soul. The newer gods are revealing new fluidities, which are connected to the old "sturdies." Rock gardens are good places to think about these concepts—a place, perhaps, to find the Bossa Nova.

# The Lucy Stoners

When I divorced in 1980, I had used the name Donna Schaper for a married life of twelve years. Formally, I was the Rev. Donna Schaper. My first husband's last name, *Schaper,* is Holland Dutch and pronounced *Skopper.* As I have said more times than I would want to admit, put an *s* on to the word *copper,* and you have it. That doesn't prevent people from calling and asking to speak to the Rev. Shaper, with a long *a*, or the mail carrier from delivering letters addressed variously as Skipper, Schapiro, Skilleppi, and the like, nor does it keep people from mumbling most of the introductions I receive. Rev. mumble, mumble will now address us on the subject of whatever.

When we divorced, I had already had a professional life under this alias for a dozen years. Almost no one knew me under my father's name of Osterhoudt. I had two good reasons to stick with Schaper: I was known that way, and Osterhoudt was twice as difficult to spell. Either way, I was borrowing a man's name.

The man I fell in love with at age thirty-four presented me with new name problems. I met Warren Goldstein (meaning gold-stone in English) at Yale while I was working there as a chaplain. He was teaching American Studies and working with a group of students who happened to meet in my office, and the rest is history. We now have three children: Isaac, Katie, and Jacob Goldstein, each with an interesting middle name—Eugene for Eugene Debs, Emma for Emma Goldman, Frederick for Frederick Douglass—none with Osterhoudt or Schaper. Yes, this new compromise bothers me. I thought about taking Goldstein because it was most consistent with my previous compromises but decided not to because of the obvious problem of being referred to as the Rev. Donna Goldstein.

So here I am—a person with no real name or with a lot of names. I could go by "Stoner"—that compromise suggested by the great feminist Lucy Stone in the nineteenth century. Stone was born in 1818 and became a powerful orator, talented organizer, and real idealist. She was purer than I am and was the first American woman to keep her birth name, even after marrying Henry Brown Blackwell. While she was called Mrs. Stone all her life, her followers changed their many names to Stoner. Stone thought women should have something of their own to go by. No doubt her reasons parallel those of modern feminists who choose to be "Starhawk" or "MorningStar." Something natural is less discriminating than something historical, in the minds of many women.

The Lucy Stoners thrived for a while, and I suppose that if I became desperate, I could have joined them. Donna Stoner has a nice ring. However, it would require a new person to go with it, and the main thing I know about myself is that the person I am is all these names and connections, not any one of them. I have never even met Lucy Stoner! I have lived with Donna Schaper for a long time, but whenever I think about the identity issues we all face, I am glad a few women solved theirs with the name of Stoner.

Your rock garden also may need a name. It may even need a plaque, like "Columcile" or "Covenant" or "Place" or "Spot" or "Rover." You may want to spend as much meditation time naming your garden as you do growing it.

# Rocks Are Places for the Spirits

The great psychologist Carl Jung argued that people "smuggle" their biography into almost everything they say or do. People also smuggle spirit into their gardens, and rocks are one of the ways they do so.

Rocks speak the language of eternity. They speak of strength. Eternity and strength are synonymous with the Spirit for many.

What is eternal, though, is change and tension. People tend

to love rocks because every now and then they give us respite from the permanence of impermanence.

For example, there is the everlasting debate—since at least the Moses-and-the-golden-calf episode surrounding the giving of the Ten Commandments—about the use of idols or statues or icons. (Rocks can become idols or statues or icons if we confuse their divinity with God's divinity.) Protestants and Catholics have been debating this for the past five hundred years. Catholics are much more comfortable using "things" to attract attention to God; Protestants are very uncomfortable with "things." They want nothing between them and their God or them and their Bible.

Many Catholics make a place for the Spirit to reside in their homes by creating sacred spaces, such as garden statuary of

saints or niches containing votive candles before symbolic artwork. Protestants stick to coffee-table books. Jews place small objects, called mezuzah, outside of their front doors. Less-religious people use candleholders made of colored glass or just a photo or a feather or a rock or two from afar placed on an otherwise uncluttered table.

Mantles deserve and receive our best objects. These may change over time—but certainly a lot can be told about a person by what is kept in the places of honor in his or her home. You can make a rock garden on a mantle and put a fresh bouquet in it every week the same way people change the flowers on their tables.

Others build an actual rock garden in one of the nooks or crannies of their yards.

Rocks carry spirit the way almost nothing else does: They cannot be destroyed. They smuggle the eternal. They are heavy and beautiful and not the work of human hands. Synthetic rock is a contradiction in terms. No human can make a rock.

# Contemporary Spirituality and the Rock

Stones could solve the paradox of contemporary spirituality. The paradox is in settling the unsettled. Robert Wuthnow, an expert on religious trends, tells us that stability as well as motion are key issues for the spiritual search. Many people today want to return to something solid but can't find it. Rock gardeners are part of that group: We don't worship rocks! We do enjoy their solidity and the way they point us to the Spirit.

God occupies definite space in the universe and creates sacred space in which humans dwell—there, knowing our territory and feeling secure. Many Americans, however, believe themselves to be movers and shakers, part of the rock and roll crowd. This tension keeps us spiritual seekers on our toes: We want to be fully grounded as long as we don't have to stay on any one ground for too long.

In the sixth century, St. Benedict asked monks to embrace both dwelling and seeking as equal parts of the spiritual way of being human. Temples and altars for worship reflect the dwelling aspect; rocks are the foundations of the dwelling spirit. The seeking aspect is expressed in our desire to be part of an unfolding process, to negotiate, to be on the road, to experience novelty, and to grow.

Rocks are perfect spiritual companions: They let seekers settle. Rock gardens can make eternal spaces in our homes or yards. Similarly, keeping a stone in a pocket lets us move with something stable in tow. Stones provide a nice paradox for the modern seekers: We get to move; yet we remain rooted. Fluidity is not all; something sturdy is also our companion.

# Fetishizing

Itzhak Bentov, the self-named metaphysical physicist, long ago argued that matter contains consciousness. Those of us who walk along beaches with rocks in our pockets know exactly what he means.

Scholars call these pocket-fillers fetishes. Putting spirit into matter is fetishizing. Some of us see the verb differently: We don't put spirit into matter. We see what is already there.

The great anthropologist Joseph Campbell believes that the

manifestation of the sacred in a stone or a tree is neither less mysterious nor less noble than its manifestation as a "God."

He is arguing for the fetish, against those who doubt the spirit in the stone. We stone gardeners don't doubt the spirituality of the stone, nor do we overdo it. We don't make God a stone or an idol. Instead, we enjoy stones as pointers to the Spirit.

Because so many of us have been educated in a Western, proscientific, promaterialist manner, we sometimes have a hard time accepting "spirit in the stone." Joseph Campbell has no problem doing so. Imagine if we had received a different education. Imagine if we had learned to embrace the spiritual *and* the material.

Many people raised in the Judaeo-Christian tradition have been taught to be very suspicious of idols. Fetishizing is not a natural religious pattern for us. We are rightly and genuinely afraid of committing the sin of idolatry.

The members of the Shinto religion join many ancient peoples in being encouraged to worship rock in a way that most of our Western religions no longer do. The Rock of Ishi in Japan is a shrine of nothing more than a large rock enclosed by a fence. People come to this rock in observance of the Shinto faith—even though no one knows for how long they

have been coming or what makes this rock so special. Obviously, rocks call people's names, and they come.

One simple way, beyond the fetish or the idol, to use our own rock gardens or mantel piles or rocks in the park spiritually is by making pilgrimages to them. We can visit them whenever and however we want—at the same time each day or once a week or in the same way at various times of the day or week, or just once every month at the full moon. Any ritualized visit is a pilgrimage. These pilgrimages help our stones to be pointer fetishes, not idol fetishes; they help us to find God.

# Shrines

Carl Jung once said that he had to make a confession of faith in stone. So did Moses. We may join their words and their pledges by creating a shrine.

If you have to break a bad habit or addiction, like drinking too much or eating too many fats, or if you want to change in any way and become a new person, stone can help you. Find your personal stone, and place it where you can see it; touch it whenever you feel the need; and renew your promise to change in its presence.

What is a shrine if not a simple holy place where we remember who we are and who our God is? Why do shrines have to be magnificent? Why can't they also be simple? A self-made altar in a yard or a park or a forest can carry us to the Holy Spirit as well as anything else. Build one, and you will understand Thomas More when he writes that "shrines make a spirit palpably present; they celebrate rather than explain and generate intimacy between the human and the more than human. . . . A shrine transfers the holiness of faith and whatever spirit is captured by sacred imagination to a particular place for memory and honor."

Big words; all they really mean is "holy ground."

# The Kitchen Rock Garden

We have a little rock garden right outside our kitchen window that gives us a place to look for God—if we are wise enough to try. We built it from scratch because there was an outside area that was kind of empty. The old New England house we bought from two master gardeners—who had lived in it only on weekends and in New York City the rest of the time and who had the services of a professional gardener—came with dozens of garden sites: perennial beds, chapel gardens, big vegetable beds, raspberry

and currant patches—enough to keep us unmasterly gardeners in constant tension about how we were ever going to keep
the place up. Nothing, however, had been done in the ten-feet-
by-ten-feet spot outside the kitchen window. Later, we discovered the reason: It had been the dog pen for the little Corgies
that the previous owners raised for years.

In the beginning, morning glories were all that we could
grow in this spot, which included a bird feeder on a tree outside the kitchen. It was as ugly as sin but as useful as could be.
Flat and already well dug in, this feeder contained seed for the
birds right at eye level, but something had to be done to dis-
guise it. Morning glories did the trick: The bird feeder wel-
comed their climb. Blues, pinks, and whites twined around the
feeder, singing an off-color version of "The Star-Spangled
Banner" right after the Fourth of July each year. They self-
seeded and called one's attention away from the sandy ground.

The morning glories have had a few friends from time to
time, but mostly they constitute the vegetation in our kitchen
rock garden. A peony is taking root at the moment as are a

few day lilies. Annual
nasturtiums have done
well because the soil is
so bad. They like bad
soil! We built the rocks
into a double ledge to
hold the sand and to
cover up the remnants
of the pen. They come
from all of our old
places: Cooperstown and
Long Island, both in

New York, West Virginia, North Carolina, and more. This year, a rock beauty has arrived from the Cape of Good Hope in South Africa. We add rocks to our garden frequently. When the flowers sing "The Star-Spangled Banner," the rocks sing, "Gonna Take a Sentimental Journey."

In our kitchen garden, the plants are less important than the stones. The stones carry the beauty. The base is made of a dozen white rocks with blue streaking from a nearby Williamstown, Massachusetts, dump. These rocks have no particular nostalgic significance. Rather, they are a good base for the grays and browns from the Long Island Sound and the blacks from Hungary. There are a few from Nice and Paris (a very few as suitcases are not friendly to large rocks) and some from Dublin. There are quite a few from the Poconos; these are slate gray. When it comes to rocks, the off-whites and off-browns and off-grays are amazingly diverse: There must be a million colors of rocks. There may also be rocks in our little garden the origins of which are totally lost on domestic history.

The rocks don't sing alone: There is a lot of competition from the birds and the flowers and the house. This garden is the one you see and smell when you get out of the car and unload groceries or reload sports equipment. This garden is a busy garden, a working garden, even though we'll never really be able to grow vegetables in it. It is the site of that late day "HAAAAA" that means: I'm home; I'm off the highway.

One year, I planted white nicotania in with the morning glories. They have a mild, delicate smell that is very unusual. I loved getting out of the car—"HAAAAA"—and closing my eyes to smell the nicotania. They also needed to be watered all the time, so eventually a certain practicality had to replace a certain luxury.

Anyone can build a large or small kitchen rock garden. We started by hauling stones from our old home near the ocean. However, any rock will do. A rock from overseas can be paired with a rock from the nearest mountain, which can then join a rock from last summer's vacation. These rocks remind us of stories and can even tell stories. Why did we pick this one over that? Because that's where the baby fell. Why did we go to this place in the first place? Because our friend, now gone, told us it was a great one. Gathering rocks from our lives' many pilgrimages keeps us connected to those pilgrimages.

Now that both the rocks and flowers in the kitchen garden are set in their ways, a loud, chirpy bird family has moved into the bird feeder. Our cat Oscar spends a lot of time hanging from a dead cedar branch. He swears he is just watching the morning glories growing—but we know different.

# STONE

A rock pile ceases to be a rock pile

the moment a single man contemplates it,

bearing within him the image of a cathedral.

—Antoine de Saint-Exupéry, *Flight to Arras*

# The First Rock Gardens

Reginald Farrer, a British-born, upper-class traveler, is widely considered the father of the American rock garden. He died in China in 1920, at the age of 40, while searching for still more of the alpine plants he called "little people of the hills." He had survived bad porters—of which he complained vehemently—angry Tibetan monks, attacks by Chinese bandits, and more. Why? Because he was enthralled by the alpine flora. He wrote in 1907, just as the rock-garden movement was getting started by his efforts,

"I am the fonder of my garden for the trouble it gives me." He also loved to caution people who endlessly and carefully photographed his garden in California that "they made it look so much more splendid than it really is."

Americans, as well as the British, were the pioneers of modern rock gardens. The world's first societies were formed on this side of the Atlantic: The British Columbia Alpine Plant Grower's Association was founded in 1921. The Rock Garden Society of Ohio was founded in 1929 and later became the American Rock Garden Society.

Rock gardens were part of the leisured, not the working, classes in America. "You can't eat a rock" was the response of many who farmed for a living. Pleasure gardens weren't really a possibility at all until people moved away from farms to towns and cities. That "urbanization" oddly brought us the garden as we know it, which was followed soon by the rock garden.

Credit for the first use of natural rocks in gardens probably goes back to the ancient Chinese who displayed their religious affinity with nature by creating miniature mountainscapes. Kublai Khan is said to have made his rock garden out of lapis lazuli. The Japanese followed by creating miniature worlds that imitated the larger world of nature that they saw. The Western world, by contrast, maintained a dislike of, or at least lack of appreciation for, "the wild" until the Romantic Movement of the late eighteenth century. Before then, we worshipped in buildings or through holy books, not in nature. We were less likely to want to worship through nature—while today the romanticization of nature can get in our way.

Rock gardens in the West began as compensation for a lost sense of the natural. As people in America and Europe

became more urban, they started to remember what they had lost. That feeling of loss should tell us some of the irony of gardening: It is about recreating nature and maybe even Paradise. We began in a spiritual garden. It is to Eden that we try to return when we garden.

As early as the 1920s, The Garden Club of America sponsored nationwide lecture tours by a renowned expert on alpines, the Swiss nurseryman Henri Correvon. Around the same time, *House & Garden* magazine regularly carried twenty-page articles by such experts as Louise Beebe Wilder. By 1935, so many rock gardens with water features had been made that public health officials in Philadelphia were warning of a possible outbreak of malaria from mosquitoes breeding in all of those pools. In 1938, New England rock gardeners spent $725 (a hefty sum during the Depression) to create a display of "right" and "wrong" rock gardens for Boston's Spring Flower Show and handed out twenty thousand leaflets on the subject to the public.

Fortunately, we are beyond such fashions. Right?

# Finding Stone

You may find that you already have a lot of rock on your property. Build to those rocks. You may be lucky in a different way and have no rock on your property: Your luxury is that you can pick the rocks you want. Plus, you get to haul them. My favorite local nursery, Annie's Garden Center, has a sign out in front of its main garden, "Annie's Fitness Center." Think of all the money you'll save on weight lifting.

Even if you don't have property at all, rock gardening is not impossible. You need to adopt a piece of dirt. There is a lot of orphan dirt around in any neighborhood. Again, there already may be rocks right there. It simply needs to be "gardened." As an alternative, you may want to make a portion of a public park or garden yours, imaginatively, and care for it with a rock or two. You might even add a plant or pull a weed from time to time.

Either way, whether starting fresh or starting fixed, you will want to place and amend stone with your own signature. You will want to choose stones from places that matter to you so that the memories of those places will adhere to the stones you use. If a place doesn't intrigue you, pick a special day— your birthday, your wedding anniversary, the solstice—on which you collect your stones. Don't just rock around: Rock intentionally.

You will be astonished at the amount of stone that is actually out there just sitting around, mostly for the taking. Look on construction sites or in the corners of mall parking lots. Look where bicycle trails have been cleared or on abandoned properties. Look near water, at the sea or lake shore, on river banks, and on the bot-tom of shallow streams. Be sure to ask permission before removing stones from someone else's property.

Between the years of 1700 and 1875, gangs of workers in New England piled stone after stone into walls. Edwin Way Teale says that by the end of the nineteenth century, there were a hundred thousand miles of stone walls in New England alone.

Many of these are now crumbling because of development and/or neglect. Quite a few gardeners are making new use of the old stone, particularly as borders for their gardens.

You may not live in a place like New England, where rock was piled up for you. You may have to go to construction sites to find and haul stones, or you may have to buy rocks from the growing number of stores specializing in rock. Be prepared to look at gorgeous stones from these dealers—and to pay a heavy price for them.

The deserts are as full of stone as the old New England pastures. I am thinking of Sedona Red Rock or the Kaibab Limestone in the Grand Canyon or Navajo Sandstone in Zion Canyon. Some of the stones in the four corners of New Mexico, Arizona, Utah, and Colorado have, at times, looked downright blue to me. Stone changes color as the sun and the day move along; stone that is blue at noon can turn back to gray by late afternoon or vice versa.

Pennsylvania slate and limestone fall incessantly on the highways. If you see fallen stone on a major route, take the next exit. Find the back of the sliding mountain and harvest a few rocks. The only limit to finding stone is your own imagination. Stone is everywhere.

# A Little Bit of Geology

The old saying "hard as a rock" has its reason. Most rocks are genuinely hard. However, some are not. There is a range of hardness of rock that includes chalk, shale, and mudstone soft. These soft rocks aren't very good for the garden because they break too easily. They disintegrate and return to soil; thus, we don't use them to build.

Geologists speak of the principle of "differential erosion." The way we tell between a hard and a soft rock is by how the rock erodes. In almost any cemetery, you can see tombstones that hold their markings and tombstones that do not. Nature is forceful: Rain, frost, and sun all have an effect on eternal words. On soft rock, those words don't last. On hard rock, they do.

Soft rock on a peak will last longer than soft rock that is on a lower cliff of a mountain. Higher is always harder when it comes to rock. On a much smaller scale, we see that there are real differences in the solidity of pebbles. How can we tell? By using a hammer to determine the order of hardness.

Most precious and semiprecious stones, as well as gold and platinum, are gathered from stream beds or beaches where nature has presorted them and let their order of hardness determine their value. Again, the principle of differential erosion is at work. The harder grains sit on top of the softer. There also are often conglomerates in these water beds—hard and soft rock stuck together in one mass. Sometimes these conglomerates are quite lovely in the garden as long as there are enough of them with enough of a blend of color and size.

Geologists and engineers are also interested in the question of how big or small rock can be. They know that there is nothing but rock under the surface of the Earth and that rock can be solid for hundreds of miles downward. We might argue that all creation is just one giant rock garden. Some poets have referred to the Earth as a pebble in the sky.

A scale of measurement was needed under these circumstances. Geologists define any rock more than ten inches across as a boulder. Stones are from two-and-a-half to ten inches across. Pebbles are smaller yet—from a half to two-and-a-half inches. Last but not least, we have the various sizes of granules, sand, and silt that are too small to stand out individually in the landscape. Most rock is broken off from other rock, so what may have started as a stone could easily become a pebble.

Thus, the question of a rock's size depends upon how it appears when unattached and unbroken. Fortunately, no one has yet made a career of measuring large, unattached boulders. These large pieces dazzle us, but we are hardly going to use them in the garden.

# The Color of Rocks

Color in rocks often comes from iron compounds. Iron is a great pigment-maker. Black, brown, red, and purple join the green that comes from traces of copper. In the desert, we often see a color known as desert varnish, which is a brownish streaking. Varnished surfaces were often used by Native Americans who pecked or painted their art on them. By what art historians refer to as pecking—breaking through the outer dark coating to expose the lighter rock beneath—the artist could achieve a pleasing and lasting cameolike image. Later artists often "wrote" over earlier ones, which gives us some evidence that several thousand years are needed for darker desert-coatings to form.

We also find varnish on pebbles. The term *valley of gems* is often applied to places of well-varnished pebbles.

Another type of "paint" occurs when strongly colored material from rocks above washes down to lower rocks. The great Red-wall Limestone in the Grand Canyon is really a formation covered with fine red silt that dripped down from a very red Supai formation up above.

Lichen can also color rock. Lichen is a lowly form of vegetation that comes in gray, green, yellow, or even brilliant orange. Old dead patches can be black or white. Lichen don't need much water: They grow with extreme slowness, and they leave scars that take on color when they fade away.

# Stone Working

The most common types of stone for big projects are granite, limestone, sandstone, and slate.

Granite is hard and dense. It can be coarse or fine grained and solid or speckled with gray, blue, or pink. Difficult to cut because it is so hard, it's generally used in walls and foundations. It doesn't like to do anything it is not already doing.

Limestone is medium-soft, and its colors range from light to dark shades. It's easy to work and cuts well, but its durability is only medium to poor. Limestone has the widest extent of colors—from pale green to gray to tan to white to black.

Slate is soft and dark gray or black. Slate splits easily along its grain and can be cut across the grain with a masonry saw. Durability is medium to poor.

Sandstone is soft to medium-hard and can be brown, gray, or red. It also has a medium-to-poor durability.

Each of these stones can be used in a variety of ways, depending on availability and the degree of fuss the gardener is willing to endure.

Most rock-garden projects can be done with the softer stones. Durability doesn't matter as much in the garden as it does in the house or chimney.

Other kinds of stones that gardeners use include basalt, which is a heavy weight that is colored gray to black, and gneiss, which is a medium weight and is colored gray to black and striped with bands of white quartz.

You may find stones containing ancient fossils or covered with colorful mosses. These can be quite delightful when placed in the right space.

Flagstone, which is a shape of stone, not a type, is very popular in the garden. Because it is sedimentary and tends to separate along its layers, it can be hard to trim. It may decide to fall apart or come apart or be split apart by sawing exactly in the way you want it to, or it may decide not to meet your desires. Its flexibility can work for or against you.

Alternating the use of small stones or gravel with large rocks is the easiest way to work with different sized stones— the kind that have a mind and shape of their own. If you add small stones to make up for the differences in stone thickness, you'll be surprised at how easy it is to get stones to dry-stack.

Dry stacking is different from wet stacking in that no cement is used. Most rock gardeners stay away from cement; they prefer the unusual shapes of stones to create the beauty. Evenness is abandoned on behalf of natural beauty.

Much stone work is a matter of revealing what is already there. A retaining wall of basalt, for example, is easy to put together if we notice a lot of large basalt stone lying around on the ground. We put it back. We reveal where it was before it fell down.

To split a stone, rest it on thick sawdust or carpet scraps or a bed of sand. To split along its grain, mark a line around the stone with a soft pencil. Then, drive metal wedges along the line, and strike each with one blow in succession until the stone splits.

When you are done, you may weep. You have split a stone. Then, build. You must now.

# Piles, Projects, and Patterns

Rocks can become gardens in thousands of ways. There are so many options. . .

Some people are experimenting with spiritual water sculptures. The most beautiful spot near my house in Massachusetts is at Amethyst Brook in East Amherst. People have built a marvelous brookside series of cairns—rock piles—that make a monument to I don't know what. I keep hoping that I can plant some alpines anonymously in their vicinity. A rock garden built anonymously, then used by the public, is a delightful idea of eternity to me.

Rock on rock in Nashwaaksis, New Brunswick, Canada, is the creation of Daryl Maddeaux, an artist who grew up playing with the round rocks of the Nashwaaksis River. He has discovered that rocks of any shape can be balanced into improbable towers. Although many imitate this art form, few have perfected the technique of balancing a heavy boulder on a tiny stone as has Maddeaux. His special interest is using his display to demonstrate to school children that nothing is impossible and also to help managers to think "outside the box."

Not all of us will need to do the almost impossible with our rocks or gardens. We may instead do the possible. If you live in an apartment, "borrow" a public space for your rock garden, your place of prayer, your spiritual niche. Pick a quiet spot in the nearest park. Find an empty parking lot. Adopt an abandoned corner. Then, start to pile stone upon stone.

If you live near the ocean, mark a part of the beach. Residents of Craigville on Cape Cod, Massachusetts, used to create an ongoing communal sculpture of stone circles right above the tide line. Some days, it was made of circles in labyrinthine form. Other days, it was made of long rows of descending-or ascending-sized rocks and stones.

If you don't really like the outdoors, stay inside. Take over a table or a dresser top with a vase and a stone. Even a windowsill will accommodate a few feathers and a matching rock.

How about a specific gardening project? We saved an old, wrought-iron scale—that had been used to weigh ducks—from a Long Island farmer's barn, just as the barn was about to be demolished for yet another strip mall. Round and large enough to hold forty ducks, that scale became the base of an outdoor fireplace. Stones came later and were placed to fit around the scale, which was a little bent out of shape—the stones had to embrace the scale just right.

That fireplace yields us a nice summer and winter solstice fire, as well as a neighborhood gathering place. One year, we lit a fire despite snow and made s'mores with marshmallows and chocolate and graham crackers.

A fireplace is a great centerpiece for a yard or garden, and rocks make it work.

You also may find yourself drawn to shells or driftwood. These beach finds have a place in a sentimentally oriented rock garden. Different types of stones and shells can cohere in silly or interesting ways: Keeping them separate enough so that they don't look too busy but connected enough so that they show a pattern is the trick. A wave design for a path, for example, can incorporate many varieties of stone, shells, or driftwood.

One gardener made a river of stone on her odd-shaped lot. She put the stones in a swirl pattern, imitating that of a bending river. It was an enormous project, but once completed, it was hard not to see water on the ground.

Getting stones to look like they flow can be difficult. The fluid effect results from arranging elongated river stones so that they all point in the same direction and overlap like fish scales. If the stones are irregularly shaped or uniformly round, sort them by size, and lay them in a subtle gradation—from the largest stones along the banks to the smallest down the center. The stones can also be arranged in swirls to suggest eddies and pools, or you can dispense with the stones altogether and spread fine gravel or sand atop coarse gravel. Then, rake the surface into ripple to evoke the serenity of a Zen garden.

A dry stream looks most effective if you locate it where water would naturally run and gravitate to low spots on the terrain. If you add a twist or bend, place boulders inside the curve, as if the rivulet had been forced around an outcropping. A tree or a shrub can also give the stream a visible reason to zig or zag. Exploit grade changes by laying large rocks across the channel to suggest a dry cascade.

Some gardeners use stones as markers and borders. The Inukshuk are stone figures made by an Inuit tribe in the Northwest Territories of Canada. They serve as signposts for travelers who otherwise would be lost in snow and ice and sky. The stones tell them which way to turn. Using a stone as a marker, a gate, or a gateway is a good idea: Not only are you able to mimic a great people, but you also have a way of notify-

ing visitors to the garden of its beginning and its end. Something is starting, and something has stopped.

Always think first about the very basics for your project. Some of the most important decisions a stone gardener has to make involve the foundation stones. Once you find the right base stone, be sure to bury it at least one-third of itself deep. That way it will look like it belongs to the land rather than like an immigrant.

Seasons, shapes, sizes, foundations—all these and more are the elements that keep rock gardeners working with stone in playful ways.

# Boughten Rocks

I think I know why people buy rocks with writing on them at a garden store. Words like *love* and *peace* are soothing and promise tranquility. Plus, there is an initial humor in the presence of a well-written, well-etched word.

I have one at the gate of my garden: It says simply *My Garden* and was given to me by a well-meaning friend who doesn't understand gardening. Gardening is about the natural, well-made—not about the well-made in *faux* natural.

These commercial rocks are a problem in the garden. They almost wear their price tags in a places where price tags are inappropriate. They are a form of advertising even for those who don't know their prices. Those of us who decant our tomato and orange juices understand. We are so compulsively afraid of what labels and advertising do to our souls that we want to avoid all tags and labels in the kitchen and the garden.

With all due respect to those who love rocks and love stones, "boughten" stones should be kept out of the garden. They mix metaphors and media in a way that bothers both. They denaturalize nature. They mix us up.

So why did I keep my boughten rock despite my aversion? Because it was a gift and thus couldn't be tossed without offense. Plus, I am not a purist. I learned long ago what a little "mixed-uped-ness" does for the soul: It keeps us humble.

# Building a Stone Wall

Stone walls can be laid with or without mortar. If you have never built one, begin without mortar, and go no more than three feet high. Because dry stone walls move with the freeze and the thaw cycles, they are more flexible than mortared ones. Dry stone walls don't need a concrete footing and require an excavation of about six inches.

Look for flat stones with a solid base, a flat top, and one or more straight sides. For wall ends and corners, you'll need a supply of stones with two flat sides that meet at close to a right angle. Large stones will speed a project along but can be very hard to handle. Most people stick to stones weighing less than thirty pounds, which make less of a statement but save the back.

A farmer once told me these guidelines for building a stone wall: "Place the course on firm, level ground, using stakes and level lines to guide the construction," he said. "Place larger, more irregular stones on the bottom, digging as needed. Tilt

the stones slightly toward the center of the wall. Plan to taper the faces of a wall inward a minimum of one inch for every two feet. Fit each stone so that it contacts the adjacent stones in as many places as possible. Place the stones 'one over two,' staggering vertical joints by laying one stone over the joint between the two below. For stability, make the wall at least two stones thick."

How did our ancestors ever learn all these details? They learned by trial and error, for sure. We could and will learn the same way.

# The Virtue of Heaviness

At my local library, I came across an 1887 farming manual titled, *Fences, Borders, and Bridges: A Practical Manual.* It showed how to build a stone wall. "Never think of rock as too heavy," the manual advised. "Weight is its prime virtue."

This little manual made three suggestions about how to work with rock: One is to throw a party. Get your friends in, and make a challenge out of it. Two is to have strategic equipment, to build levers. Three is not to move stone at all but rather to build around the good pieces. The manual said the best place to begin a border is where the biggest stone lies.

I took only this third piece of advice. The advice proved good. I have my big stone sentimentally ensconced in an unlikely place. Instead of a mass of bramble, young trees, and anonymous shrubbery in the southwest corner of my property, I have a rock garden in the making. In that corner, I can remember all of the virtue I hauled—and all the stories those stones are remembering with me.

There are at least two ways to look at rocks. One is clearly in the spirit of heaviness. How will I ever lift that stone? The other is lightly: The rock will move when the rock needs to move. Operate on rock time, not clock time, when it comes to the rock garden. Then, big levers, or even big parties, will matter appropriately to you: When you and they and the Spirit are ready, the rocks will move. Until then, the rocks will stay put.

People can insert anxiety into anything, even into the rock garden. Of course, such anxiety is completely unnecessary. However, that doesn't stop many of us from trying to get blood out of a stone or coals from Newbury.

I like to say this sentence often: "What the Spirit wants, the Spirit gets." The opposite is also true.

Alice Walker once wrote that she has a "love affair with tiny wildflowers and gigantic rocks." When we have a love affair with rocks, we don't rush them. We let them transform, slowly over time. We want to share every developing minute.

One of the great things about rock gardens is that no one has yet written the definitive guide to them. They are versatile, unvaried, small, large, sunny, shady, specialized, or a smorgasbord. We still have freedom to enjoy our own piles of rocks, whether they be light or heavy.

# Stone Rolling

Stone rollers are in good company. After all, someone is said to have rolled the stone away from Jesus' grave. Rock gardeners have the same bargain with eternity: We participate in it.

We make changes, ironically, all the time by putting in big, sturdy, unchanging rocks. Then, we move them or watch their colors change in the rain or their shapes emerge in the snow.

We participate in a certain seasonal renewal. We count on change, eternally and rigorously.

I am thinking of the way E. B. White described his beloved Katherine as she aged but still knelt to plant bulbs in the November wind. "As the years went by and age overtook her, there was something comical in her bedraggled appearance ... the small hunched-over figure, her studied absorption in the implausible notion that there would be yet another spring, oblivious to the ending of her own days, which she knew perfectly well was near at hand, sitting there with her detailed chart under those dark skies in the dying October, calmly plotting the resurrection."

An anonymous writer wondered recently whether Mary Magdalene was really mistaken about Jesus in the garden: "When Mary Magdalene mistook Jesus for the gardener, was she altogether wrong?" This writer loved gardeners so much that he or she thought of Jesus as his or her equivalent or at least as gardeners as very dear to him. They make beauty where they go.

Rock gardeners are not capital $R$ resurrectionists, but we know a little about the little $r$. We participate in simple ways in miracles. We watch stones roll away all of the time.

# Margins

Except for the most naturalistic variety, good gardens have good borders and good margins. The writer Tillie Olson spoke of her life needing margin. She had run out of space; her life had run into the walls of her frame. Artists and photographers insist that the empty space around an object defines it as much as the filled-in object itself. It is almost always a good idea to halve any garden once you have planned it. Every year, a rock garden

will need a good pruning and airing: Be sure you give it one, or you will end up with clutter instead of peace.

The same thing is true of life: We need margins. We need space. We need to redefine what is in and what is out. We need to simplify and trim down—precisely so that we can complexify and fill up again.

Boundary lines are key to a rock garden: We need to see them and not let them go blurry. Gardens have to begin and end somewhere; otherwise, they become a bother. They need inside space and outside space.

For most of their history, humans used stones to differentiate inside space from outside space. Stonehenge might be the most obvious of such structures. People have long needed a way to mark in from out and to know what belongs to inner and outer, private and public, and mine and yours. Stones are simple tools for the gardener: They alert us to what is inside and what is outside.

# Secret Gardens

Nobody knows it's there, but I do. Many gardeners have a private space deep within the already private spaces of their gardens. It is a spot that they prefer to all others. We won't admit to it out loud, nor will we show it to even our most intimate visitor. However, inside we know where we go when we really need a place *to* go.

A secret garden is often a place to which we return when nothing but a good cry will do. It is the place we touch good-bye when we go away on a long trip. I always put garlic peels in mine: I want its immune system to be the strongest possible one in the whole garden, and many bugs despise garlic.

If something were to happen to the cosmos that grows in this little place, by virus or mold or any of the garden's many enemies, I would feel hurt myself. It wouldn't just be the plants. Thus, I add the garlic peels. I protect this inner space from intruders of all kinds.

Adding a stone or taking one away is something I find myself doing in this little place. Why? I don't know. Yet move the stones, I do. They seem to like it. Perhaps I move them because I know something is moving inside me. I don't go to the secret garden unintentionally.

I don't know if I will ever do anything big with or to this spot in gardening terms. I don't want any harm to come to it, neither do I want it to be so fancy as to require much work. I simply like knowing it's there, doing nothing, waiting for me to find a new place for an old stone.

# PLANTS

When I get depressed,

I go and watch the stonecutter

hammering away at his rock,

perhaps a hundred times

without so much as a crack in it.

And then on the hundredth and first blow

the rock splits in two

and I know that it was not that one blow that did it.

But all that had come before.

—Author Unknown

# Her Obsession

Acknowledging that most rock gardens are built when a homeowner has a landscaping problem—an eroding slope, a granite outcrop in the middle of the lawn, a swimming pool that needs to be tied to the garden landscape, awkward changes of grade around a split-level house, or a boring yard with no changes of level at all—master gardener Joan Means lets out the real secret of rock gardens: They are too easy. Once you start, you can't really stop, because the very lack of effort needed to maintain what you have becomes embarrassing. They solve landscaping problems but do so in too easy a way. Once you terrace with rocks, nothing much more needs to be done. Once you lay down the rocks between the lavender plants, they stay. Like a beautiful face with good bones, a rock garden, well begun, stays beautiful. Rocks and low-maintenance ground covers are an obvious answer to many a garden problem, and if you stop with them, you have a rock garden. However, most people don't know when to stop. Obsessive gardeners are at grave risk. I join Joan Means in self-describing as obsessive. We get carried away and don't know how to stop. We end up with way too much of one thing, like dwarf rhododendrons or dwarf daffodils. Although I really don't know how anyone can have too many dwarf daffodils.

Rock gardens confront the same problems as people do. We go too far when just a short way will do. If you have ever played much tennis, you know what I mean. Missing the easy shots is why most of us lose most games. Simple stuff can be the hardest of all. A simple spiritual observance, like carrying a rock in your pocket to remind you of God and/or of the fact that you are breathing, can almost come too easy to the genuine sinner. Sin boldly, say the rocks; or at least, that is what I hear them saying. Sin simply is their follow-up line.

# Patience

The very first step for a beginning rock gardener is learning patience.

Process is more important than product, and even the easiest plants to grow take ten days to brave the outside world and another thirty or more to flower. Some of them will show up season after season (the perennials); others (the annuals) will come in seventy- to ninety-day life spans, and that will be that. You cannot rush a flower. You cannot rush a bloom. The best way to trick the flowers out of their mortality is to plant in succession: Put daffodils in for the spring, day lilies in for the summer, and perennial mums in for the fall. That three-season background of color will allow lots of annuals also to strut their stuff. If you are lucky enough to be a four-season gardener, just keep in mind how much those of us in the shorter seasons envy you. Then, consider a similar strategy: Succeed by succession.

Lots of people will try to tell you that they are not "gardeners." I think they just don't know how to start. "I am not a gardener," they will say. "I am not spiritual," they also will say. They are wrong. Statements like these are like guards standing at the gate of heaven: On behalf of Paradise, we could walk right by them.

If you want to start a rock garden, there are three basic practical matters you have to consider: One is soil, another is light, and the third is stone. There is only one spiritual matter —patience. The garden will not grow to its full maturity tomorrow; it may not even grow to its full maturity for years.

May Sarton, the gardener and essayist, said in her long essay on solitude: "It does not astonish or make us angry that it takes a whole year to bring into the house three white peonies and two pale blue iris. It seems altogether appropriate that these glories are earned with long patience and faith."

She is right. The garden owes us nothing—and yet, here come the flowers. There lay the stones.

May Sarton may know less about patience than she makes out. She used to drive some readers quite crazy with her impatient urgency about solitude and patience in the garden. On the one hand, she seems to have more friends and guests than anyone else. On the other, she seems quite unhappy to have them. She frets. If it rains the day after *M.* comes, then how will she get the daffodils in? "The dianthus will spoil if we don't get more rain. The dianthus will spoil if we get too much rain." If she didn't write such successful books, then she would not have so many successful correspondents, and if she didn't have so many successful correspondents, then she wouldn't have so little time in the garden. Her trouble mimics this winding, whining language. The garden brings her peace; the friends hassle. So why does she spend so much time with the friends and so little time in the garden? If there is an answer, Sarton will find it and fret about it.

Most gardeners will lust for an ever-more-beautiful garden —and more beauty requires more patience. Many gardeners join Sarton in going to the garden to find the patience they don't find elsewhere. Katherine White (the wife of E. B. White, who wrote *Charlotte's Web* while she worked as the first fiction editor of *The New Yorker* magazine) was an overly productive person. She managed the magazine and its various writers, a famous husband, their children, and a sparkling literary life. Then, as she and *The New Yorker* aged together and more time was at hand, she began to garden. Her husband described her as mingling manuscripts with seed and bulb, editing Amos Pettingill of White Flower Farms with the same dark pencil that she used on Thurber. Pettingill was the owner of her favorite seed supply company; she used to write to him about the bad style in his catalogs. Often wearing a suit, she came out of the garden looking as officious as when she entered it. Her greatest gardening pleasure was the arrangement of the flowers for lunch. Once an editor, always an editor.

Katherine lusted impatiently after the product of the garden, its beauty, the filling up of space with colorful peace. She and May Sarton both give endless descriptions of windowsills cradling blossoms, of eyes that can't write unless they are graced with flowers. Both were greedy and impatient for these flowers, but the garden taught them the patience of waiting. This paradox about patience—that it is both the heart and the turmoil of starting a garden—keeps many would-be gardeners from ever starting. We seem to know that the garden won't be all we want it to be immediately. It may not ever be all we want it to be. Surely, more than one joke has been told about the people who show their gardens on local garden tours. The standard comment is, "Oh, if you could just be here tomorrow when the irises are fully open," or "You should have been here yesterday before the peony petals began to fall." The garden teaches patience precisely because each moment is so *big*. We become impatient for those *big* moments. Unfortunately, or fortunately, the only way to achieve those moments is through patience.

# Light

beginning rock gardener can have all the patience in the world, but if he or she doesn't have good light, nothing much will be accomplished. Plants can't grow in the dark. I have a tower of four clematis that had to be moved three times. This year, on the far west side of my property, they finally decided to bloom. Light is essential to plants, and they are very picky about getting it. If they don't get it, they won't bloom.

Finding the light is easy: Once we know how essential it is

to our garden, we simply go for it. Siting a garden after we know the pattern of the sun in the high-growing season is absolutely the most important thing to do. Watching the sun's course over your property is a fun thing to do—and must be done over time, not for just one day. Of course, you can plot the pattern by scientific advancing of the dawn-to-dusk cycle, but you will have more fun timing it through personal observation.

Rock gardens often take plants that enjoy shade more than other plants. The rocks seem to go with the darker corners of plots. If moles have dug holes in your lawn, perhaps that is the place to sneak a rock garden. If a ditch marks the end of one corner of your property, that very indentation may be the place for rocks to "grow." Yet, rock gardens do not require shade or corners or holes—they can be made where you want them to be. Beginning a garden requires only that you know what you want to plant. If daisies are what you want to grow, you'll need sun. If you want violets, you won't need as much. If Shasta—the many-colored green plumes that line most shady spots in America—are your cup of tea, then shade will do.

To make your decision about flowers and plants—which is oddly the easiest choice in gardening—simply look on the package or ask the grower to determine the amount of hours of sun the plants will need to thrive. I have made more mistakes with irises than anybody I know, mostly because I keep putting them in spots without enough sun in their high-growing period. They became lovely and green but didn't flower. The clematis and the irises have teamed up against me. I have learned my lesson: They are now in full sun.

At Sissinghurst in England, Vita Sackville-West's castle home, her unconventional gardening ideas tested the capacities for sun and shade. She liked to say that she pushed her plants to their edges in terms of light. She had more than one unconventional idea, but we should never forget that she was a master gardener. She could afford unconventional ideas. She practiced a kind of ruthlessness in her gardens, never keeping a plant that didn't work. Hers was an unplanned garden, a spontaneous garden, one in which wild experimentation was always taking place. Her famous gardening columns for *The Observer* of London endured from 1947 to 1961, showing that she had plenty of new ideas to carry on.

When we start out, we usually can't be so free. We might not have anything left if only the perfect are allowed to survive. In addition, I would rather cut off my thumb than throw out a plant, and many other gardeners are equally thrifty. Thus, the importance of light: You don't want failures; you want plants to thrive.

# The Oddball Success

One reason to garden is for the oddball success; the humorous reappearance of the impatiens growing up, not where it was planted at all, but instead through the stones in the walkway. How was it that no one stepped on it or noticed it till it bloomed? Also, aren't impatiens supposed to be annuals?

If you have ever tried to grow them from seed, you'll know what I mean. They are not easy to grow, but this one grew up on its own. This one reminds us that we dare not plant or prepare for everything in the garden. What control we do exert is positive: to make the greatest possibility possible.

Gardeners tell the most wonderful stories about the plants that reseed themselves. One had spent $70 one year on new astilbe for a spot next to the raspberries only to discover that the delphinium had decided to come up there by seed. The astilbe, of course, died.

Let the garden surprise you. It will.

# Off-Season

Every northern gardener knows that there are some days in which nothing can be done in the garden. Blizzards, hail storms, thunder—each eliminate garden activity. The gardener is wise to have a plan for these days so as not to have compulsions uprooted. James Lipton wrote a book called *An Exaltation of Larks*. On nongardening days, we may "exalt" our stones. We may look at them from memory or from under an umbrella. We can enjoy them. We can memorize them. We can count them. We can joy them.

The way of life of a rock plant is to get its roots underneath the rock for coolness and moisture. They are working even if we are not! They root slowly. We can exalt them by watching them root slowly. Maybe, we can even root slowly ourselves.

In the winter, when it is not too cold to garden but really nothing much can be done, consider mulching as a pastime. Putting down only half of the winter mulch (not on iris, they love a mulch–born leaf disease) in October gives us something to do in November. Removing half of the mulches early in March gives us something still to do in April.

In between mulching projects outside, start a rock garden on a windowsill indoors, with lots of plants and a few stones.

One of the great off-season pleasures is that of reading about gardening. At our local dump—a place of no small satisfaction—I picked up an entire box of old gardening magazines last winter. They dated from the forties and fifties; their edges were browned by age. I read one issue an evening and was bereft when my box was emptied.

Another off-season pleasure is planning and plotting (graph paper is a dreamer's delight), not to mention buying seeds. I like to list all the bulbs and seeds and garden paraphernalia I could possibly want and then "lose" the list for a couple of weeks. I then order a third of what I thought I needed, fully aware that I still will have way too much, no matter what.

Winter can be full of loss for those who must have dirt under their fingernails all year round. The rest of us can compensate by the off-season pleasures of the imagination—or by moving to one of those wonderful climates with four outdoor seasons.

# Three Sure Plants

One is hen-and-chickens, (*Sempervivium,* meaning "always living"). If you can't grow these plants, you can't grow anything. They reproduce like rabbits and manage to do so under just about any condition—dry or wet—and in almost any kind of soil, but overall they prefer light and dry. They show a great diversity and color, and mixing the species is often a dramatic experiment that works. These plants used to be called roof houseleek, from their habit of nestling happily on European country thatches. They reproduce by offsetting little imitations of themselves.

They are ideal for odd spots like crevices and stone walls. To plant them in unusual places, put a little molasses on their root systems, and just stick them in (no kidding). My favorite is the cobwebb houseleek (*Sempervivium arachnoideum*); I love the name as much as I love the plant.

Hen-and-chickens has several species native to Mexico. Some are flowering versions. These often involve rosettes of leaves, often with red markings along the tips. They love sun and are succulents, so never overwater; the soil must go dry before watering. They grow very close to the soil line, but as they age, they develop stems. With time, the stems grow taller and taller. Every now and then, the plants will flower. The rosettes are always clustering at the top. They are very eager to root and will grow quickly.

The value of hen-and-chickens in a rock garden is the way they sneak through crevices to grow—always doing something unusual and unique to their spot. As part of my prayer life, I like having such images to work my own problems through. Sneak through the crevice, I hear God say to me, and grow!

Another sure hit is mother of thyme (*Thymus praecox*). It makes a grayish, pink carpet and has pink flowers in summer. It does well in limy soils and full sun and may be grown from seed or cuttings or by division. The only problem with thyme is that it may take over the whole garden.

Dozens of dwarf bulbs come to mind for the rock garden, but none is so certain as the dwarf daffodil. A few small hybrids are February Gold, February Silver, and Tete-a-Tete. What is great about these plants is that they will come up before everything else when we are deeply hungry for color in the garden. They will announce the rest of their friends—and we will admire their courage in late winter/early spring.

# Tricky Plants

Ladyslipper, alyssum, morning glory, strawberries, candytuft, cheddar pinks, geraniums, heathers, phloxes, and scilla all do well in most rock gardens. Be careful of saxrifages and gentians: They need sand, and they need a little breeze. They don't flourish in the restricted, tamped-down soil of rock ledges. Henri Correvon, a famous rock gardener, thought these latter little ones were best grown in the crevices of a dry retaining wall, where they can find a breeze and be placed in a microclimate that they will enjoy.

Many rock garden plants are endangered and threatened. If you experiment too far outside of the normal nursery, you'll want to be sure that you are taking special care to keep things alive that might be threatened. You'd be surprised how many people don't know what they really have in a rock garden —especially in an inherited, older one.

When purchasing wildflowers from a nursery, always inquire about the plants' origins. Be sure that you are purchasing plants that will do well in your particular garden area— that they were grown originally in microclimates similar to yours.

Every community has a good nursery. A good nursery has employees who have stayed around for a while and who know their business. They know plants and what is valuable, endangered, rare, or in need of special care. I recommend befriending one or two nurseries and sticking with them, precisely so that they can help in the identification of unusual plants.

If you have inherited a garden and can't identify what you have—in either Latin or English or in your native tongue, find the best nursery owner you can or the oldest member of the local garden club. These experts will know what you have and will help you to care for it.

# Arranging and Expanding the Rock Garden

A rock garden often enjoys one big plant right in the middle or on its best edge: That plant "thematizes" the rest of the space. I like hydrangeas and sages in rock gardens. They have a presence and take well to small friends.

My neighbor, on the other hand, has made a delightful theme in her rock garden by using a circle of chives, which flower on purple tips in the spring. These tips blend into pink at their stems. This blending contrasts with the long skinny green legs of the chives themselves. Placing the slenderness in a circle gives interest to shape as well as color.

She "bought" the chives from herself by dividing in the fall. You might want to do the same. Arranging the garden is often a matter of knowing what you already have and using it well.

Keeping plants within the family is a source of great pride for a gardener, but it may result in disease (God forbid its arrival), wiping out everybody. A little genetic and plant diversity goes a long way to keeping our "garden portfolios" varied enough to survive a storm. The advice about borrowing from oneself only goes so far—we also need to bring in "immigrants" for the garden to stay healthy.

# Hostas and Heathers

Hostas are a great friend to the shady rock garden. They have a great shape and love to be divided and to grow and fill up an entire area. They make an especially attractive pathway because they line up well. Hostas can be separated in the fall and will take a year or two to return, but when they do, they will make a long, lush border. Mature hostas quickly make a humble property feel and look "rich." They are grand—and spiritual wealth doesn't mind a little grandness to touch off its essential simplicity.

Divide hostas from the clump. Work a spade under the rhizomes, and lift the whole clump. Then, divide them cleanly with a knife. One big hosta clump can produce three new plants. Each will have a nice cluster of roots and at least one bud.

Hostas do bloom with long white shoots in the summer. A good variety is Bressingham Blue, which has outstanding foliage, color, and texture. Its flowers are fragrant and usually come in June. Its name alone is worth the planting. Another interesting variety is *H. undulata,* which has bright green leaves with crisp white edges. It has lilac flowers later in the summer. There also are smaller hostas like Golden Tiara, if space is a consideration.

For a fancy rock garden, consider heaths or heathers. Heather has evergreen, and often colorful, foliage that gives the garden year-round interest—even during the bleakest month of winter. Growth habits range from the small to the large. A low-maintenance plant, heather needs only annual pruning and mulching to promote vigorous growth. Heather is a common name used quite loosely to include both heath *(Erica)* and heather *(Calluna).* They include over one thousand cultivars that include many different shades of gray, gold, yellow, and orange.

# If You Want
# Flowering Plants

$\int$ome favorite plantings for

rock gardens include the primrose, which is clearly the gem of

the rock garden because it requires so little space. The English

primrose *(acaulis)* bears a single flower on a short stem; the

*polyanthus* has clusters of flowers on a longer stem. The *gar-*

*ryarde* is a short-stemmed *polyanthus* hybrid from Ireland that

has unusually dark foliage, while the *juliana* is a creeper that

thrives in rocky crevices. The creepers are my idea of survival specialists. They remind me of Jacob, as they find and make and keep a place to live. Like Jacob, they use rock as a pillow and dream great dreams of the holiness of their own crevice.

For a more mixed garden, early tulips can be good. Likewise, minidaffodils, scilla, and lobelias have good carriage. You might also use arabis and golden alyssum, aubriettia, violas, polyanthus primroses, forget-me-nots, pansies, or English daisies. All of these are for spring bedding and need companion plantings for other seasons.

Stay clear of big things, like caladiums or coxcomb or canna or *Begonia rex*. They overpower the rocks. The same can be true of prayer life. The large is often dangerous to the Spirit.

Finally, good plants can be borrowed from the forest floor. Consider Eurasian wood, columbine, forget-me-not, *Myosotis sylvatica*, Dutchman's breeches, bloodroot, foam flower, any of the sedums, and wild blue phlox.

Because rock-garden plants are so congenial and grow so quickly if they like their location, they will almost always find their way from a neighbor's yard to yours. If you are only going to live in a place for a short while, and you know it, making horticultural friends is terribly important. They will remember you by what you took from their gardens and made grow in yours. They will even tell the next property owner the story. I have some magnificent red raspberries that still have a now-deceased friend's name on them. He gave me two sticks one fall. The patch now covers a quarter of an acre and is still marching toward the sun.

# Weeding

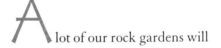A lot of our rock gardens will

be untended, even unnoticed. They will also "borrow" seed

from birds, and thus plants will arrive that no one expected.

Each fall, as I clean out the garden, I see how the seeds attach

to my pants just to survive and be resewn. I know most of

these seeds: They are just little fighters, nothing grand at all.

Thus, my garden prayer: "May all your weeds and seeds be

rare wildflowers."

If they are not wildflowers, be prepared to do a lot of

weeding. Grass is the nemesis of my rock gardens: I have to weed a lot to keep its ugly straightness from cluttering up my space. The grass is ugly only to me and my weak hands but not to nature. Those seeds that stick to my clothes manage to live.

Getting to know the difference between a weed and a flower is not always easy. It takes some practice. Usually, the gardener's rule of thumb is that if it pulls out easily, it's a flower. If it pulls out with difficulty, it is a weed.

Weeding is a part of soil-work for most gardeners because it is easy to let a weed get established and hard to get rid of it once it is.

In Riverhead, New York, on the corner of Northville Turnpike and Route 58 was an enormous field. It was probably the most accessible open space within walking distance of my old house, and so I went there a lot. I learned weeds from wildflowers there, and I harvested pockets full of seed.

I also grieved there because the town was in the process of giving that old corner to yet another strip mall. The strip mall now stands; a few of the plants, thank God, will also make it. I know they will. The wildflowers I chose as well as the weeds, which stuck to me and took a trip off their reservation, will survive—both, not either. Resurrection means the victory of some weeds over some strip malls. Even gardeners don't get to decide which will live.

Before concrete took over the field, something new was happening there every season. It brimmed with St. John's wort, daisies, dandelions, crab grass, Timothy, clover, pigweed, lamb's quarters, buttercup, mullein, Queen Anne's lace, plantain, and yarrow. It sprouted grasses too numerous to name— but each did have a name. Not one of these species was there before the Puritans landed. Like most Americans who live in this country, each is an adaptation. The peculiarities of their adaptations make for the best eulogies.

Weeds are as unlikely a source of affirmation as we can mention—and yet, and yet, they have a kind of particular magic, and they also carry a message. According to Sara B. Stein's botany book, *My Weeds,* wild oats growing in a field of alternating furrows of spring and winter barley will mimic the habits of either crop, depending on the row. She also tells of a rice mimic that became so troublesome that researchers planted a purple variety of rice to expose the mimic once and for all. Within a few years, the rice mimic had turned purple, too.

The botanical fact about weeds is that they grow in response to human disturbance. The more that humans disturb the environment, the more weeds adapt and grow. Botanist Jack Harlan writes in *Crops and Man,* "If we confine the concept of weeds to species adapted to human disturbance, then man is by definition the first and primary weed under whose influence all the other weeds have evolved."

Ralph Waldo Emerson would have agreed. He said that a weed is simply a plant whose virtues we haven't yet discovered.

We come to the garden alone, while the dew is still on the roses and on the weeds and on the rocks. There, we interact. Some part of our being lives on, poking through the concrete of the progress that tries to obliterate us. Other aspects of our lives are remembered, spoken, and articulated as eulogies. Then, we are gone; the rocks remain.

# In a Public Place

If you are like me at all, you dead head lilies in the park, meaning that you pull off the dead flowers to make way for the new ones, or you pluck off seed pods from flowering cosmos at the playground and "arrange" rocks and plants that aren't exactly yours. Why not? The beauty is yours and then some. Short of quarrying a public area, there are lots of ways little rocks can be moved around in a playful way to enhance the beauty that is sometimes hidden. I think especially of debris, which often has rock in it. Move the rock to a corner if needed, or let it play with other rocks. Use what is there; don't import! If rocks have fallen out of their places, ask another passerby to assist in placing them back where they belong. A falling stone wall is not pretty. A stone wall is.

You may not be the kind of person or may not have the opportunity to build a stone wall either in public or in private. However, you can plant bulbs if you can kneel, and there is simply no grander combination of color and shape than a good old stone wall with daffodils naturalized in front of it.

I often plant daffodil bulbs on property other than my own —especially if the stone wall is particularly dilapidated or destroyed. The daffodils lift it from despair.

If you don't have stone walls in your immediate environs, you probably do have flowers that transplant well. I am think-ing of pea vine or morning glory seed. All daisies love to travel in a pocket from one locale to another—especially after they have flowered and have formed their seed pods.

I have kept a "life list" of the good walls and the good daf-fodils. I'm up to seventy-four—and making more as the days go on. The bulbs cost only about thirty-five cents each, and you can spend an entire weekend making your region more beautiful for less than a hundred dollars. I know. I did it once. Three here, three there—and I get to go back and see how they've spread.

# Stumped

I had been stumped by that stump one gardening season too long.

The big oak had fallen a decade ago, and because the stump is on the far end of the garden, I didn't mind it too much. I looked around it. I looked past it. I made believe it belonged to the neighbor. I asked the tree people for a price to remove it, and each came in close enough to $500 to warrant my continuing neglect.

Still, every year its half-excavated stumpish root called to me in insulting words. "Blot," it sneered. What bothered me most was the stalactite nature of the wood remaining on the old thing: Evened off, it might have been pretty. As it was, it was not.

Two years ago, I threw morning glory seeds at it the way hippies used to stuff guns with flowers; the way my daughter mulches, using leaves as fairy dust; the way my son wipes dishes, sort of, half way, tentatively. I tossed a molehill at a mountain.

Guess what? The stump has disappeared. It is covered with blue flowers in the morning and the rest of the day, with green foliage. No one knows its unevenness is there. "Smart," it calls out. Easy. I feel victorious—in an Easter sort of way. The way the good architects tell us to build to the land's trouble, I built a centerpiece out of an eyesore.

The effort was find-
ing the seed, which
was easy enough, as I
have morning glory to
spare on this property.
However, I borrowed
a lighter blue from the
farmer down the road,

on two accounts—one was that I liked his color better than mine, and the other was that his plants were extremely healthy, having climbed his whole barn.

I am no longer stumped by my stump. It still sits there in the off-season; but starting midsummer, it blossoms. The rocks that now circle the old stump help to hide it, and they mulch the morning glories.

Presto. Magico. Unstumped, and a new rock garden exists.

# If You Hate Sermons,
# Skip This

We preachers know more about stumps than most people. Christians actually claim to derive as a people from a stump, the stump of Jesse. My garden has given me more sermons than any other sources, so forgive me if I tell you a little more of what I know about stumps.

The day after Thanksgiving last year, our neighbor obtained a pass for the vicinity of the ghost towns at the Quabbin Reservoir, which provides water to Boston by underground pipe. The ghost towns were in the way of the city's thirst, thus, their demise so that the reservoir could expand. These ghost towns are now fully underwater, but one can still travel the pastures that used to surround them. There are old, beautiful stone walls on these pastures. While admiring these walls, some of which were as tall as we were, we actually saw the biblical tree, the stump of Jesse; or so we think.

The stump had fallen out of an enormous fir tree that had a terrible gash in its south-facing side. It had dropped a piece of itself. God only knows how. The dropped piece had rooted in the ground. It had a little fir tree, looking for all the world like a Christmas tree, growing out of its "stumpedness."

God has a great sense of humor. From any root, God can branch.

Things grow from the inside out as far as God is concerned. Things don't always grow in a regular way. They grow any which way they want to grow.

This is not true all of the time, mind you. I bought a magnificent jade plant for three dollars at a yard sale two years ago. The woman who had owned it for twelve years was moving to Florida. What she had kept alive, I destroyed. In the same way some people just can't find a good job or a good spouse or a good perch, I couldn't find a good window for that plant. It rotted out from its very core.

God may grow a tree from a stump. God may grow things irregularly. I can't even grow things in the regular way sometimes.

What is interesting about the biblical understanding of growth is that it sides *with* the unnatural and *against* the nurturing—not *with* the natural, *and* not *with* the nurturing in the great nature/nurture debate—but differently, almost strangely. Growth is odd according to the Bible. Many of us believe that a good environment raises a good child; a bad environment doesn't. So we pay enormous attention to what windows we put our flower children in. We turn them. We water them. We put Miracle-Gro™ fertilizer on them. Some of them turn out just fine. Some of them stay stumped for a long time, only to flourish when they feel like it. Still others become jaded. (I am not just making a joke.) We all know the astonishment of a well-watered, well-placed child rotting from the roots up. Conditions for growth are often a matter of some difficulty.

There is a near command from many sites in scripture to nourish our roots so that we may branch, so that we may flower, so that we may live a fullness of life that is unstumpable.

We are to grow from the inside out—not from biofeedback in. In the promise that growth can come—even from deep within a stump—we can find two or three useful points of view for our own lives. One is almost silly: We aren't dead yet! Sometimes we may feel like we are, but we're not. We may be dormant. We may have been overwatered or put too many times "where the sun don't shine," but we're not dead. We may have very little we do well. We may have grown, like an old apple tree, into a funny, twisted shape. However, as long as we do just one thing well—like play well with others or pick up our crayons—we aren't dead yet.

The stump in my garden is dead, but it can bear life of another sort—an odd sort. No one thinks of oak trees and morning glories as having a natural affinity. What they have in my garden is an unnatural affinity. Gardeners *do* interfere with nature.

Another consequence of the scripture is this: If the promise is that growth can come, even from deep within a stump, and that growth is inner, not outer, then imagine what we have to look forward to as a people. I don't know about you, but I find the outer world increasingly demonic and petty. The temples seem to be well described as being in the great nap instead of in the great awakening. The times stink. We seem stumped. We seem to have been stumped for a long time. The axe is laid at many trees. The children suffer.

What this means, of course, is that a dive to the depths is in order. We may pierce the old dead wood for its vigor. If we aren't dead yet, and our nation is not dead yet, and our houses of worship only look that way, imagine what it would be like to think like a stump. Think like a Quabbin stump. Something awful and strange happened to the tree that dropped a large part of itself to the ground. I can't imagine what, but the image of Jesus' crucifixion surely comes to mind.

The tree at the Quabbin Reservoir grew anyway. It grew irregularly. It branched from its root. The same is true of my problem stump. The tree died too soon. I can't wait for it to rot naturally: That will take hundreds of years. Having it removed would take hundreds of dollars. Morning will have to show its glory through its corpse. The great stone walls will stand by.

# SOIL

Behold this compost! behold it well!

Perhaps every mite has once form'd part of a sick person;

yet behold!

The grass of spring covers the prairies,

The bean bursts noiselessly through the mould

in the garden,

The delicate spear of the onion pierces upward,

The apple-buds cluster together on the apple-branches. . . .

—Walt Whitman, "This Compost"

# Ground Level and Below

The importance of soil rivals light when it comes to rock gardens. What happens underground is just as important as what happens above. The soil is tremendously important from a chemical viewpoint. You can have great light and great patience, great siting and great feng shui, but if you have bad soil, you're sunk. The most important thing any gardener can do is build the soil. This soil-building work is the winter work of the garden, and it is a lot of fun. Making compost—out of my own kitchen scraps, restaurant kitchen scraps, my neighbor's kitchen scraps, as well as leaves, grass clippings, hay, and the all-important and all-humorous manure—is so much fun for me that I think I enjoy finding all of these soil enhancements as much as any other aspect of the gardening work.

Eliot Coleman, one of the premier American organic gardeners tells us that "there is more life below soil than above it" and "the secret to success in agriculture is to remove the limiting factors to plant growth." These practices do that by efficiently and economically generating a balanced soil fertility from within the farm rather than importing it from outside.

Soil depth should be considered in three ways, by touch, by sight, and by how far you can dig in it. Soil depth equals how deep you can go with a shovel before hitting something that won't let you dig any farther. Great soil lets your fingers walk down its depth; average soil requires a shovel. Three or four inches down are needed for a rock garden—much more for a vegetable garden.

When I go on a garden tour, I always put my hands in the soil and get my fingernails dirty. If the soil moves, it is probably good soil. If it balls up or cakes, it is probably not good soil. Some think the best soil is "balanced" soil with equal acidity and alkalinity; I think not. The best soil has the pH that the plant you want to grow there needs.

The best way to get good soil is to amend soil: Add compost, manure, sand, and vermiculite until you get the feel you want. Then, use a soil tester, which is a pH stick. Follow the instructions, and you'll know what the soil's chemical status is where you touch it. Remember that just because the south end of your plot measures seven on the pH scale, it doesn't mean that the north end will measure seven also. Take two or three sitings, and then plant.

# Compost

How to make compost in two sentences: Layer scraps (no animal scraps) with leaves and grass or hay and manure, and then layer some more. Turn the pile as often as possible to give it air.

Good soil builders are like eager beavers. We are always building soil. We don't finish ever building it. We are simply always at it. We know that the dirt-black sheep manure of five years ago is no longer active in our garden; it needs to be replaced with new, good stuff.

Don't go to a dinner party without bringing home the scraps: Your garden will reward you next year. I actually bring home the lobster remains from the lobster dinner at our summer family camp. The tomatoes love fish heads as well as lobster. The calcium in the bones is a real bonus in the soil also.

Building soil is a grand and life-giving event. We are literally leaving the earth in better shape than we found it. We are stopping the *awful* waste of this culture. Acre by acre, we are stemming the loss of topsoil, which is one of the great environmental problems.

Winter is the best time to build soil. However, we need to be careful not to lose the fallow, quiet period in the garden by working too hard on this. Even so, we may slowly, carefully amend the goodness that is already there.

For those of us condemned to live where snow and ice accompany winter, rock gardens are a constant source of inspiration. They give us winter work and winter beauty. They don't change as much as season themselves. In spring, a few yellow daffodils in front of a big rock remind us of nothing so much as the cold time, the time when rock and snow collided in a comforting picture. When green dances with the rock that used to dance with the snow, we are reminded of why we planted rock in the first place. We did not want to be bereft of winter beauty.

Good gardeners can't just sit still in the winter:

We want to think we are making some contribution to the ground while enjoying its often-stunning winter costumes.

Joseph Wood Krutch, the great nature writer, said that the only thing he didn't like about New England was February, but that's because he didn't know March. March is mud. March is gray. March is snowless. March is long. However, even in March, which is an honorary member of winter, rocks display beauty. They look even better when wet—and wet does not seem to bother their spirits. They persist as themselves. Rock endures, even in winter.

# The Largest Pile

One winter, on the morning of a "big" meeting at work, I found myself standing on top of the largest pile of horse manure in South Amherst, Massachusetts, laughing my head off, as I slowly made a dent in it.

I often don't go to work too early if something is happening later in the day. I want to conserve energy. By gardening early —even in the winter—I find that I can keep myself alert for those low-sugar hours between 4:00 and 6:00 P.M. This way, I bite fewer people's heads off than I might otherwise.

I had been searching for a good pile of manure for snow layering since the late fall. I don't believe in growing tomatoes without an excess of farm manure. If you get in the fresh manure by January, it is delightfully ready for June planting time around here.

For some reason, I wasn't finding much manure at all. I figured I was in serious competition with the hundreds of other gardeners in my little spot in Eden. "They" had gotten to the good stuff. "They" had already hauled it off to their own plots and were already reaping the great benefits of manure on snow on manure on snow. The seeping of the stuff into the ground is a winter tea with high nutritional merit, according to the "old folks." I always liked putting the manure on right before a new snow to honor the folk wisdom.

I also imagine that the physics of a slow melt allows the kind of leeching that good soil builders like.

So on this day, I was driving along a country road near my home when I spotted steam rising straight to the sky. With that much steam, at 15°F, the mother load could not be far off. There it was. Almost as high as the horse barn. I careened in the driveway, almost hitting the white cat, the gray cat, and the mucker-out-of-stalls, who skimmed her shovel, flannel shirt, and boots out of my greedy way right at the last minute. I asked her if I could have some manure. She said, "Sure." I couldn't have been happier.

I backed my van all the way down the long dark, mahogany-laden horse corridor and stuck its end right up against the pile. I remarked privately at how odd it was to be putting manure back into a rear end, but that was what I was doing, and I was delighted at the convenience. (I have hauled manure longer distances.)

The coincidence with my "big" meeting was not small. As I mounted the pile, I thought of the memos, the revised memos, the revisions of the revised memos, as well as what my political adversaries probably were going to do this afternoon to the revisions of the revisions of the revisions. The higher I got, the deeper I got. I was in excrement twice as high as my own height. I was in excrement as wide as my house. I was in the biggest pile in South Amherst.

My pride knew few boundaries. "They" didn't have this.

Then, she told me. First, came her flannel shirt, then her glinty shovel, then that look in her eye that said she was so much more accustomed to shit than I. "Get it while you can," said she. "'They' come tomorrow from the college to take it all."

I could have wept. I didn't. I have some self-respect left inside my own flannel shirt and behind my own shovel.

How much could I haul in just one day—even if I skipped the meeting—three vans full, maybe four? Could the garden take all of that?

My accomplice on the tall pile showed me the best stuff on the north side of the pile—on the far end. I took it, raced back home, put it on my garden, and went on to my meeting. What was my laughter's source? It was from what I knew would eventually come of all this stuff. I even had a glimpse of hope for the meeting. It, too, was a serious contender for one of the largest piles around, and I could have all of its compost that I wanted.

# Manure

Obviously, if you are just starting a garden, you might have to buy compost in bags. If the expense of that is too much for you, simply talk a farmer into dropping a load of manure on your site and wait six months. That will cause better soil and teach you patience.

If you are gardening in a very small space, be careful not to overdo the addition of manure or compost. Think in terms of 1 percent manure, not much more, unless the manure is very old and friable.

If you live in the city, you may want to donate your kitchen scraps to the community garden's pile. That urban trek can be good for the soul and for the soil.

In a garden of any size, the soil needs to be turned annually, and the new compost needs to be dug in. I believe in a complete manuring every other year, and I find that such a manuring, joined with annual composting, works quite well. If you live at the ocean, use seaweed as your manure. If you live in the suburbs, get to know the greengrocers and the fishmongers. You may have a hard time talking the neighborhood into a manure truck's arrival, but you will be honored for your thrift and foresight by other gardeners.

I have a friend who brings me all of the outer lettuce leaves from the local Italian restaurant: First, my chickens eat the leaves, and then I get their manure. Lettuce breaks down very quickly, and restaurants across the country throw away outer lettuce leaves.

Coffee grounds are good if you want to acidify your soil, and obviously, they are everywhere as well. If you have nothing else to do, sprinkle coffee grounds on your raspberries or blueberries. They will thank your January activity next July, at breakfast.

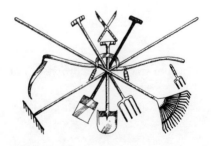

# Soil Is Not Just Compost

$S$oil is a combination of dirt and air. Aerating the soil sometimes requires digging. In rock gardens, there is very little digging because so many of the plants are perennials and shouldn't be disturbed and because often the spaces are very small. A little "tickling" (loosening of the soil) to add air is better than a lot of digging. Just lifting the soil sometimes can give a very refreshing breather for both plants and soil.

When first digging a new plot, however, it is important to

double-dig. Midge Ellis Keeble, one of the great garden writers of all time, describes double-digging in *Tottering in My Garden* as follows: "Instruction: excavate the entire bed to a depth of two feet. I shall pause here to allow time for reeling around and protesting."

Double-digging or French-digging is basically the replacement of all the soil two feet down with all the soil from the top. Double-digging takes a long time and a good back. The double part means that you bring the bottom to the top, and then you dig it in. A rototiller can do the job better if your plot is big. Back to patience—there is no reason why you have to dig the whole site on any one day.

# SOUL

So Jacob took a stone, and set it up as a pillar. And Jacob said to his kinsfolk, "Gather stones," and they took stones, and made a heap; and they ate there by the heap.

—Genesis 31:45, 46

# Ancient Scriptures

Scriptures join gardening in being full of meditations on stone and rock.

Stones figure variously in a large number of biblical stories. Sometimes, they are building up; sometimes a stronger force tears down even their strength. The spiritual gardener will know that the life of stones is double—that sometimes we build them up, and sometimes we tear them down. People who do yoga or tai chi know the same rhythm: Always work both sides; never work only one.

Never think of gardening as simply the life cycle: It is also the death cycle. It is also the "down" side. When thinking of gardening, remember both rhythms. The universe really is expanding and contracting at the same time, or so say a number of physicists.

So say the ancient scriptures, too. Stones serve as memorial markers (Gen 28:10–22 and Josh 4:1–10); places of refuge (Exod 33:20–23 and 1 Kgs 19:1–18); instruments of death (Lev 24:14, 1 Sam 17:49, John 8:2–11, and Acts 7:54); and the cause of stumbling (Isa 8:14–15, Rom 9:32–33, and 1 Pet 2:7–8). Simultaneously Jesus is called the cornerstone (Matt 21:42, Acts 4:11, and Eph 2:20), and Peter is the rock upon which the church is built (Matt 16:18).

The Ten Commandments are written on stone. The runes are holy words scratched in stone in old Scandinavia. Cliff-dwelling sculptors in the southwest wrote in images on rock, telling the stories of what mattered to them. Shamans danced inside circles of well-placed stones. Stones are said to cry out with the stories of faith, both as texts and as writing surfaces.

Consider Isaiah 26:4 "Trust in the LORD forever, for in the LORD GOD, you have an everlasting rock." Think about designing a garden around the theme of trust.

# Inherited Rocks

When my in-laws began to de-accession their belongings, I was very grateful. Beautiful things from their international travels came our way. Chinese murals, Filipino wooden sculptures, Indonesian fabric brightened our very domestic house.

My mother-in-law had long been a docent in the Gem and Mineral Division at the Smithsonian Museum of Natural History. It never occurred to me that she filled her suitcase with rocks wherever she traveled. Thus, when she gave us the rock collection from Newfoundland, Russia, and Africa, I was deeply moved. All the rocks were small, and each was a gem of a gem.

I had to find the right, very small place to put these jewels. There were about three hundred of them. They now rise in a rather distinctive heap on the north side of my largest rock garden. I put no plants in with them because the rocks themselves are too intricate.

I did take two and put them on little pillows, which someone had made and which I had picked up at a thrift store. One stone was jagged and blue; the other smooth and red. The theme of this little activity was to remember the night Jacob had used a stone for a pillow, according to Hebrew scripture. I wanted to remember how nice it was to have a home, in-laws, and parents—stones and all. I keep these displayed next to my bed as meditation objects as I go to sleep—not every night, no, but just often enough to be reminded to dream.

# Meditation

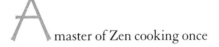 master of Zen cooking once wrote: "Throw nothing away. Balance meals. Your faults are your best ingredients." These meditative seeds are good for life and good for the gardener. Rock gardeners work with what they have—especially because often there is no choice. Some granite is not going to be moved. Some rock is not going anywhere at all. Why not turn it into a cathedral?

A gardener is someone who interferes with nature. Repent negative interference; rejoice in positive interference. We positively interfere when we respect the ways of the garden and the ways of rock; we negatively interfere when we remove a big stone only to stare at a big hole for a year or two. Work with—not against—the rocks in your garden.

Thomas Jefferson said, in 18??, that he was too old to plant trees for his own gratification. "I shall do it for posterity." If you have room for posterity in your garden, good. If not, count on there being Jeffersons, still, somewhere. Martin Luther also knew how to think in this garden way. He swore that he'd still plant a little apple tree today if tomorrow he had to die.

Think like a garden. Go ahead. Try. You will find yourself having children and reproducing all over the place from your very own stock. My delphinium have taken over all around us: We have colonized the whole neighborhood.

Meditation often requires a kind of repetition or chant. We may want to meditate using other's poetry or scripture in the garden. A good example of a garden poem on which to meditate is from George Herbert, the English clergyman and poet who lived at the time of Shakespeare:

> *Teach me, my God and King, in all things thee to see,*
> *And what I do in anything, to do it as for thee.*
> *All may of thee partake; nothing can be so mean, Which*
> *with this tincture, "for thy sake," will not grow bright*
> *and clean.*
> *A servant with this clause makes drudgery divine; Who*
> *sweeps a room, as for thy laws, makes that and the*
> *action fine.*
> *This is the famous stone that turneth all to gold;*
> *For that which God doth touch and own cannot for*
> *less be told.*

# The Stone in the
# Backyard Labyrinth

Labyrinths are archetypes found in many ancient sites, the earliest notation of which (2400 B.C.E.) is in a cave drawing in what is now Egypt. A labyrinth is a maze with only one pathway leading into and back out of the center, so there are no wrong turns and you can't get lost. You will find the center if you walk the path.

Labyrinths were used frequently in medieval cathedrals to symbolize the great pilgrimage to Jerusalem. Many use the path as a walking meditation today.

The labyrinth in our backyard started as a rumor, escalated into a whisper, exploded when a fax arrived, and came into fruition with a lawnmower. We still don't know why we built it. As much as we would like to get to Jerusalem, we probably weren't using this activity as passage. We were simply amazed by this maze. We knew it had genuinely deep religious meaning, but for us, curiosity prevailed over soulfulness.

The rumor was that a friend had the plans for the labyrinth that was etched in the floor at the Cathedral in Chartres, France. The whispers were around the dinner table: "What if we put a facsimile in the back yard?" The friend sent the plans over the fax. That very day, Warren, my most unspiritual but nevertheless very nice husband, started measuring. A few hours later, he was mowing. He mowed the shape of the labyrinth in the yard and placed a rock smack dab in the middle of it.

Three hours after that fax had come through, we had a labyrinth in our back yard. It barely fit in the big meadow behind our house—but it did fit.

The children walk it. The neighbors walk it. The dogs walk it, irregularly. The center rock grounds it.

Now, we just have to keep mowing it.

# Zen Gardens

Zen seems particularly friendly to gardening. I believe this is due to its deep interiority and calm and its willingness to use the small symbolically. In Zen as in the garden, less is more. Small is big. Paradox plays the corners.

A classic Zen garden is comprised of rocks, a plant or two, and sand, which is drawn on by gardeners-participants. Spirit is invoked in this process of change. Change is given permission; change is actually the companion of the living. We are

*supposed* to change. Often in the Abrahamic religions, the great eternities become more than a little rigid. They deny the seasons on behalf of a great monotheistic "oomph" at the beginning. Zen masters, on the other hand, speak of developing pattern, of change.

Thus, Zen gardens change all of the time: The gardeners garden them by redrawing the sand and stone. Motion matters.

The famous Zen gardens include one at Kyoto in a temple belonging to the Mashing school of the Rinzai, a branch of the Zen sect famous for its *karesansui,* or rock gardens. It is large, actually thirty meters wide and ten meters deep, and contains fifteen rocks arranged on the surface of white pebbles in such a manner that visitors can see only fourteen of them at once from whichever angle the garden is viewed. Only when you attain spiritual enlightenment as a result of deep Zen meditation can you see the last invisible stone with your mind's eye. This garden exemplifies the marriage of meditation and stone for which Zen gardens are known: As we change, the garden changes before us.

Chinese gardeners have used rocks to build grottoes and long walls, but they also let a rock stand by itself. Most prized are the pitted and convoluted rocks taken from the bottom of Lake Tai Hu. These are often seen as art all by themselves. Twelfth-century artist Mi Fei so respected one of these stones that he called it his "elder brother," while the modern poet Chuin Tung believed that when stone is endowed with personality, one can find it delightful company.

*Suiseki* is the Japanese art of miniature landscape stones that have naturally weathered into aesthetically pleasing shapes. The Japanese have been collecting them for centuries, but the art has only become popular in the West in the last few decades. Many Suiseki suggest mountains, islands, and waterfalls. Others resemble human or animal figures or are prized for their colorful and abstract textures and patterns. Collected in the wild, on mountains and in stream beds, and then displayed in their natural state, these stones are objects of great beauty. They are also sophisticated tools for inner reflection that stir in all who see them an appreciation of the awesome power of the universe and the way it shapes us over time.

# Rocks for Others

Making a rock garden, as a group or community project, as a gift, or as a memorial to something important that people experienced together, is a wonderful way to turn rock gardening's difficulty into an asset. The greatest challenge is the hauling: Rocks are heavy, and one person's back only goes so far. But, as in the famous hundred-monkeys story, if a hundred people carry one rock each, a garden goes in pretty quickly.

Rocks and flowers can accompany many happy group occasions: "I would like to build a rock garden for you in honor of your wedding," I told a friend recently. His eyes welled with tears. He was glad at the very thought. Such a unique gift certificate can go a long way to treasure a friendship, and maybe if you are lucky, the bride and groom will help you after they get settled. Relationships change when people marry. You may want to change with them and have new occasions for growth.

# Honoring Stone

Native Americans have long feared the destruction done by white settlers. Listen to an old Wintu holy woman speaking about the needless destruction of the land on which she lived.

> The Indians never hurt anything but the White people destroy all. They blast rocks and scatter them on the ground. The rock says, "Don't. You are hurting me." But the White people pay no attention. When the Indians use rocks, they take little round ones for their cooking... How can the spirit of the earth like the White man?... Everywhere the White Man has touched it, it is sore.

We will know that we are rock gardeners when the earth forgives us. When the rocks speak to us the way they spoke to those from whom we can yet learn, our real forebearers on this land.

Tatanka-ohitika, or Brave Buffalo, was a prominent Sioux medicine man of the Standing Rock Reservation, as had been his father. In 1911, Tatanka-ohitika, at the age of seventy-three, described his dream of the sacred stones. (Large stones were objects of worship among the Sioux.) Tatanka-ohitika spoke of *Wakan tanka,* the Sioux term for the higher being that is the source of all things. *Wakan* means mysterious, *tanka* great.

> In all my life I have been faithful to the sacred stones. I have lived according to their requirements, and they have helped me in all my troubles. I have tried to qualify myself as well as possible to handle these sacred stones, yet I know that I am not worthy to speak to Wakan tanka. I make my request of the stones and they are my intercessors.

If one as great and experienced as Brave Buffalo in the matter of stones and the Spirit can be so humble, it should not be hard for you or me.

The sign of the true presence of the Spirit is almost too simple to see: It is known by the presence of humility. If someone tells you they have a great spiritual garden or a great spirit, be suspicious. If someone tells you they are on their way, by the intercessions of even the stones, believe them. They have had a glimpse of the holy. They may even have learned something from their ancestors.

# Eternity

Everywhere we go, whether to the Great Wall of China, the stone circles of Europe, or the pyramids of Egypt and Mexico, eternity is marked as the rock. Rock is the best metaphor we have of everlastingness, and modern people in particular need to place rock around them. We need reminders of how long we and our children will last. Putting flowers, which fade, on top of rock, which doesn't, is a great tribute to eternity and its eternal fluidity!

It is no accident that we buy a stone for a loved one who has died and plant small flowers next to it. One simple and practical idea for a gravestone is to place three seasons of flowers in the ground. Something as simple as mums in the fall, daffodils in the spring, and blue cornflowers in the summer will work, especially if the stone carries its own weight in the winter. We don't need to "romance" the stone to know why stone comforts: It stands, and it withstands. It stands and withstands change. It rocks and rolls with us, not against us. That's why.

As John Vivian puts it so well in his introduction to *Building Stone Walls,* ". . . rock is as near a definition to forever as exists." He credits gravity with keeping rock sitting on top of itself. I credit larger spirits—the spirits within the stones that we need to address the permanent. Foundations may be slipping, but the rocks are still there, almost begging for the reconnecting spirit of the householder.

At funerals, we see the flowers. Afterward, as the flowers die, we see the stones.

# Night Gardening

I garden at night because I work all day and because I have an absurd discipline requiring me to touch soil daily. I count a day lost in which I don't tend the garden. By that I mean—on a bad day, touching it and pulling two weeds; on a good day, giving a few minutes to some worthy plot. This discipline has kept me alive to the soil and has allowed what would otherwise be an unmanageable garden to be unmanageable in a more interesting way. The discipline keeps my garden in the category of prayer: It is my rug. If I can't get there five times a day, I can bow to it at least once.

If we think of gardening as work and work only, it is very hard to do good work in the dark. If, however, we think of gardening as play—as taking our five senses out for a walk—night is actually better than day. We smell better, see more of shape and form, can still steal a piece of kale or lettuce if we want, and so on. Night gardening prohibits work and lets us play.

The most beautiful gardens in the night are the rock gardens. They pick up light; they make big spaces bumpy. They love starlight and moonlight. They are anything but dark at night. Instead, they glisten. Rather than thinking of all rock gardening as work, we might think of rock gardening along the lines of Psalm 42: By day the LORD commands his steadfast love,/ and at night his song is with me,/ a prayer to the God of my life (v. 8).There is a division to our days: Rock gardeners can work all day in their gardens and play in them at night, with or without electrified light.

Often in the darker seasons of fall and winter, I find myself moving rabbit manure at twilight or pulling up stakes at midnight or hoeing while the moon comes up. These are all done ritually as opposed to functionally. I make no claim for fertilities added or earned by night gardening, but I know that an Aztec or Mayan would. They would garden at night for the benefits; I do it for the conveniences. They would see spiritual advantages in it, but those advantages for me are of a different kind. They would find divine harmony; I find multitasking.

In the 1300s in Europe, the belief circulated widely that humans were wiser when the moon is waxing, and, therefore, any work needing thought—such as planning a layout— should be done then. Before that, Greek and Roman gardeners believed that the moon affected plants because the sap would wax and wane with the changing phases of the moon. Today, we know that tides and moons are connected. Then, they only assumed it. More than one person plants by horticultural horoscope, which strikes me as just another way of stating personal convenience.

Surely more majesty was deposited during creation than we could ever in our scientific mode imagine. There was more order, more intention, more interplay in the genetic disposition of things than even prayer and praise can comprehend. When I plant at night, after a long day of other kinds of work, I am connecting my life to these original mysteries. I am insisting that soil touch me, that night and day differentiate me, that the daring of creation be something I remember. I am a pilgrim back to that second day, when darkness was given the name of night and light the name of day.

My days are otherwise a conspiracy to make me forget that I am created, ordered, intended, even genetically mysterious. In the day, gardening reminds me of the enormity of creation. At night, with the stars as my guide, I am creation's participant-observer, kin to the divine, illuminated, recreated. Plus, usually by midnight, all three of my children are asleep!

Certain constellations have compelled the human mind since the beginning of time. Some say that science and mathematics had their origins in the questions posed by the night. No doubt religion has its own settling of accounts with the questions of the night. By day, I work on these questions as a minister. At night in my garden, I co-create when I'm not just sitting quietly, gazing at the stars or being held spellbound by the moonlight or imagining the time, once again, when gardening will be as natural as my day job.

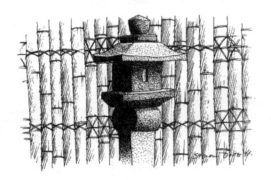

# Notes

*Page 2:* Robinson Jeffers, "To the Stone-Cutters," *The Selected Poetry of Robinson Jeffers* (New York: Random House, 1941).

*Page 17:* Quote is from *The Qur'an,* Surah 17.1. Isra', *"The Night Journey, Children of Israel."*

*Page 18:* K. A. C. Creswell, *A Bibliography of the Architecture, Arts and Crafts of Islam* (Cairo: AUC, 1961).

*Page 24:* Alice Stone Blackwell, *Lucy Stone: Pioneer of Woman's Rights,* 2nd ed. (_____, 1930).

*Page 31:* Ishtak Bentov, *Stalking the Wild Pendulum, On the Mechanics of Consciousness* (New York: Bantam, 1979).

*Page 40:* Antoine de Saint-Exupéry, *Flight to Arras* (New York: Harcourt-Brace, 1989).

*Page 42:* Reginald Farrer, *My Rock Garden* (Pawlet: Theophrastus, 1907).

*Page 64:* Alice Walker, *Horses Make a Landscape Look More Beautiful* (San Diego: Harcourt, Brace and Jovanovich, 1984).

*Page 66:* Katharine White, *Onward and Upward in the Garden.* Introduction by E.B. White (New York: Farrar, Straus & Giroux, 1979).

*Page 76:* May Sarton, "An Observation," *As Does New Hampshire.*

*Page 84:* James Lipton, *An Exaltation of Larks* (New York: Grossman Publishers, 1968).

*Page 99:* Jack Rodney Harlan, *Crops and Man,* 2nd ed. (American Society of Agronomy, 1992).

*Page 110:* Walt Whitman, "This Compost," *Leaves of Grass* (New York: Fowler and Wells, 1956).

*Page 112:* Eliot Coleman, *The New Organic Grower's Four-Season Harvest: How to Harvest Fresh Organic Vegetables From Your Home* (Post Miles, Vt.: Chelsea Green Pub., 1992).

*Page 122:* Midge Ellis Keeble, *Tottering in My Garden* (Willowdale, Ontario, Canada: Firefly Books, Ltd., 1990).

*Page 130:* F. E. Hutchinson, *The Poems of George Herbert* (London: Oxford University Press, 1961).

*Page 138:* Wintu holy woman, *Touch the Earth: A Self-Portrait of Indian Existence.* Compiled by T. C. McLuhan (New York: Pocket Books, 1972).

*Page 139:* Tatanka-ohitika, *Touch the Earth: A Self-Portrait of Indian Existence.* Compiled by T. C. McLuhan (New York: Pocket Books, 1972).

*Page 141:* John Vivian, *Building Stone Walls* (Charlotte, Vt.: Garden Way Publishing, 1976).